NEW JERSEY TEST PREP
Reading Comprehension
Common Core Workbook
Grade 3

© 2014 by Test Master Press New Jersey

All rights reserved. No part of this book may be reproduced or transmitted in any form or by any means, electronic, mechanical, photocopying, recording, or otherwise without prior written permission.

ISBN 978-1500451790

Reading Comprehension, Common Core Workbook, Grade 3

CONTENTS

Introduction   4

Reading Comprehension Exercises
Set 1 – Literary Texts   5
Set 2 – Informational Texts   15
Set 3 – Literary and Informational Texts   25
Set 4 – Literary and Informational Texts   35
Set 5 – Paired Literary Texts   45
Set 6 – Paired Informational Texts   51
Set 7 – Literary Texts   57
Set 8 – Informational Texts   67
Set 9 – Literary and Informational Texts   77
Set 10 – Literary and Informational Texts   87
Set 11 – Paired Literary Texts   97
Set 12 – Paired Informational Texts   105

Answer Key   **111**
Set 1 – Literary Texts   112
Set 2 – Informational Texts   114
Set 3 – Literary and Informational Texts   116
Set 4 – Literary and Informational Texts   118
Set 5 – Paired Literary Texts   120
Set 6 – Paired Informational Texts   121
Set 7 – Literary Texts   122
Set 8 – Informational Texts   124
Set 9 – Literary and Informational Texts   126
Set 10 – Literary and Informational Texts   128
Set 11 – Paired Literary Texts   130
Set 12 – Paired Informational Texts   132

INTRODUCTION
For Parents, Teachers, and Tutors

About the Book

This workbook will develop the reading comprehension skills that students are expected to have, while preparing students for the state tests. This workbook covers the skills listed in the Common Core State Standards. The focus of the book is on developing reading comprehension skills, but the complementary writing and language skills are also covered.

Ongoing Reading Comprehension Practice

The aim of this book is to give students ongoing reading comprehension practice without the stress of long passages and question sets. Each set contains four short texts with questions, or two texts in paired sets. By completing each set, students will gain experience with a range of passage types, become familiar with common question types, practice understanding and responding to texts, develop confidence, and master Common Core reading skills.

Developing Common Core Reading Skills

The state of New Jersey has adopted the Common Core State Standards. These standards describe what students are expected to know. The reading standards are divided into two areas: Reading Standards for Literature and Reading Standards for Informational Text. This workbook includes sets that focus only on literature, only on informational texts, and mixed sets that cover both. The workbook also includes sets with paired passages, where students synthesize and integrate information from two texts.

Introducing Core Skills

Each passage in this workbook includes a Core Skills Practice exercise that focuses on one key reading, writing, or language skill. These exercises will introduce students to the key skills and help students transition to the more challenging Common Core standards.

Preparing for the PARCC English Language Arts Assessment

Students will be assessed each year by taking a set of tests known as the PARCC assessments. This workbook will help prepare students for these assessments. The reading comprehension skills developed are those that will be assessed, so the strong skill development gained will help students perform well on the assessments. The workbook also provides experience understanding, analyzing, and responding to passages, as well as practice answering selected-response and constructed-response questions.

Reading Comprehension

Set 1

Literary Texts

Instructions

Read each passage. Complete the exercise under each passage.

Then complete the questions following each passage. For each multiple-choice question, fill in the circle for the correct answer. For other types of questions, follow the instructions given. Some of the questions require a written answer. Write your answer on the lines provided.

Robot Boy

I am not a real robot, but it is very fun to pretend. My father and I painted a box with silver paint. I glued on bottle tops for buttons. Then my father cut out two holes for my arms. Finally, my father made a large hole to put my head through. I put the box on over my clothes, and I looked just like a real robot.

I enjoy wearing my robot suit outside, in my room, and on the swing. I even wore my robot suit while eating dinner. It was hard to get the food in my mouth because I couldn't move my arms easily. I've decided I won't wear my robot suit to dinner anymore. I'll just wear it when I'm playing.

Make Your Own Robot Suit

1. Find a box large enough to fit your body in.
2. Paint and <u>decorate</u> the box any way you like.
3. Cut a large hole in the top that your head will fit through. The rest of the box will sit in your shoulders.
4. Leave the box open at the bottom. This is where your legs will go and will make it easy to walk around.
5. Cut two armholes at the front of the box.
6. Put on your robot suit and have fun being a robot! You might want to walk stiffly like a robot would or talk in a robot voice.

CORE SKILLS PRACTICE

How can you tell that the narrator enjoys pretending to be a robot? Describe **two** ways you can tell that the narrator enjoys being a robot.

1. *He says it's fun to pretent beging a robot.*

2. *He wears the robot suit when he swings, outside, in his room, and while he eats dinner.*

1   What is the second paragraph mostly about?
    - (A) What the narrator does with the suit on *(selected)*
    - (B) How to make a robot suit
    - (C) What the narrator eats for dinner
    - (D) Why the narrator likes the robot suit

2   Write the numbers 1, 2, 3, and 4 on the lines to put the steps in making the robot suit in order from first to last.

    _2_ Glued on bottle tops
    _1_ Painted a box silver
    _3_ Cut armholes
    _4_ Put on the suit

3   Why does the narrator decide not to wear the robot suit at dinner?
    - (A) Because it might get dirty
    - (B) Because it was hard to eat *(selected)*
    - (C) Because he could not sit down
    - (D) Because his father asked him not to

4   Which step in "Make Your Own Robot Suit" are the narrator and his father doing when they use the bottle tops? Circle your answer.

    Step 1   (Step 2)   Step 3

    Step 4   Step 5   Step 6

A Special Day

Dear Diary,

Today, I went with my friends to get a library card. I had never had a library card before. The librarian asked me to sit in a special seat. Then she took my picture. She printed out a card with my name and photo on it. Then she used a strange machine to cover the card in plastic. She told me how I could use the card to borrow up to four books at a time.

I was excited to borrow my first books, but it wasn't as easy as I expected. The library was filled with so many books that it was tough to decide on just four. I walked from shelf to shelf for ages trying to make my choices. Should I read fiction or non-fiction? Did I want to read an adventure book or a funny book? I didn't know where to start!

The librarian must have felt sorry for me because she came over to help me. She also reminded me that once I bought them back, I could take out another four. It's hard to believe that so many books are just waiting there ready to be explored. I think I'll be visiting the library many many times.

Brin

CORE SKILLS PRACTICE

Brin describes how the librarian reminded her she could bring the books back and take out another four. Explain why this would have calmed Brin.

When she comes back and returns the four books she borrowed she can take four other books she wants to read and this can keep on going.

1. What does the librarian do right after printing out the card?
   - Ⓐ She explains what the card is for.
   - Ⓑ She gives the card to the narrator.
   - Ⓒ She covers the card in plastic.
   - Ⓓ She puts a picture on the card.

2. If the passage were given another title, which title would best fit?
   - Ⓐ My First Library Card
   - Ⓑ How to Make a Library Card
   - Ⓒ My Favorite Library Book
   - Ⓓ A Strange Adventure in the Library

3. What does the first-person point of view most help the reader understand?
   - Ⓐ How Brin felt about her day
   - Ⓑ Why Brin decided to get a library card
   - Ⓒ What a librarian does
   - Ⓓ How the books in a library are organized

4. Which point made by Brin does the photograph best support?
   - Ⓐ Brin was only allowed to borrow four books at a time.
   - Ⓑ The library had a large range of books to choose from.
   - Ⓒ The librarian helped Brin because she felt sorry for her.
   - Ⓓ Brin had to get her own library card before she could borrow books.

The Car

This week, Mom got a brand new car. Her work gave it to her so she can drive around and meet with customers. She showed it to our family so proudly. She explained that it shows that her work really values her. She told me it was like getting a gold star on my homework. Even though it is her work car, she also gets to use it to drive us around. She told me I have to be careful when I am in it.

On the way home from baseball practice yesterday, I had a bottle of water in the car. I forgot to put the lid back on when I was finished drinking. When we went around a corner, the water spilled all over the back seat. I thought Mom might be upset and yell at me, but she didn't. She said she was just glad it was only water and not soda! Mom handed me a towel and I dried the seat. It was like nothing had ever happened. I am going to have to be more careful in the future though. I wouldn't want Mom's bosses to get mad at her, or think that she doesn't look after her car.

CORE SKILLS PRACTICE

The title of this passage is "The Car." A better title for the passage would describe what the passage is about. Think of a new title for the passage. Write the title below, and then explain why it would be a good title for the passage.

Title: _____

_____

_____

_____

_____

_____

1 Which sentence best shows that the narrator is careless?

  Ⓐ *On the way home from baseball practice yesterday, I had a bottle of water in the car.*

  Ⓑ *I forgot to put the lid back on when I was finished drinking.*

  Ⓒ *I thought Mom might be upset and yell at me, but she didn't.*

  Ⓓ *She said she was just glad it was only water and not soda!*

2 What happens right after the narrator spills the water?

  Ⓐ He dries the seat with a towel.

  Ⓑ He gets yelled at by his mother.

  Ⓒ He drinks the rest of the water.

  Ⓓ He puts the lid back on the bottle.

3 Which sentence from the passage contains a simile?

  Ⓐ *She showed it to our family so proudly.*

  Ⓑ *She explained that it shows that her work really values her.*

  Ⓒ *She told me it was like getting a gold star on my homework.*

  Ⓓ *Even though it is her work car, she also gets to use it to drive us around.*

4 What does the simile identified in Question 3 best show?

  Ⓐ How much the car is worth

  Ⓑ Why it is important to look after the car

  Ⓒ What the car will be used for

  Ⓓ Why the mother is proud of being given the car

Mother Knows Best

I wanted to eat
my dinner in bed.
My mother said,
"Eat at the table instead!"

I did not listen.
I should have thought twice.
Now my bedroom is home
to two hungry mice!

CORE SKILLS PRACTICE

Many poems involve cause and effect. The cause is the reason for something. The effect is what happens. Answer the questions about cause and effect.

What was the effect of the speaker not listening to her mother?

_____

_____

_____

_____

How might things have been different if the speaker had listened to her mother?

_____

_____

_____

_____

1. What does the title of the poem suggest?
   - Ⓐ That the speaker should have listened
   - Ⓑ That the mice are a problem
   - Ⓒ That eating in bed is a bad idea
   - Ⓓ That the mice will have babies

2. Read this line from the poem.

   I should have thought twice.

   The phrase "thought twice" means that the speaker should have –
   - Ⓐ argued about it
   - Ⓑ taken more time to decide
   - Ⓒ eaten in two places
   - Ⓓ had lunch and dinner in bed

3. What is the rhyme pattern of each stanza of the poem?
   - Ⓐ All the lines rhyme with each other.
   - Ⓑ The first and last lines rhyme.
   - Ⓒ The second and fourth lines rhyme.
   - Ⓓ None of the lines rhyme.

4. How does the speaker most likely feel about eating in bed?
   - Ⓐ She wishes he hadn't done it.
   - Ⓑ She thinks it is funny.
   - Ⓒ She is angry about it.
   - Ⓓ She is glad that she did it.

5 What do you think is the main message of the poem? Use information from the poem to support your answer.

Reading Comprehension

Set 2

Informational Texts

Instructions

Read each passage. Complete the exercise under each passage.

Then complete the questions following each passage. For each multiple-choice question, fill in the circle for the correct answer. For other types of questions, follow the instructions given. Some of the questions require a written answer. Write your answer on the lines provided.

Mozart

Mozart is a famous German composer of the classical era. He is also known as Wolfgang Amadeus Mozart. He has composed over 600 pieces of classical music. These include works for the piano and violin, as well as whole operas.

Mozart began composing at the age of just 5. At this time, he wrote small pieces for his father. He continued to learn and write music all through his youth. When he was 17, he worked as a court musician in Austria. He was given the opportunity to write a range of musical pieces. Mozart left Austria in search of better work, and lived in Paris for over a year. During this time, he was unable to find work, but he still continued writing music. He then moved to Vienna. Mozart wrote most of his best-known work while living in Vienna. He died at the age of 35 in 1791.

CORE SKILLS PRACTICE

The passage describes how Mozart lived in several different countries. Write a summary of the countries Mozart lived in and what he did in each place.

_____

_____

_____

_____

_____

_____

1 In the sentence below, what does the word <u>composed</u> most likely refer to?

He has composed over 600 pieces of classical music.

- Ⓐ   Playing a song
- Ⓑ   Writing a song
- Ⓒ   Singing a song
- Ⓓ   Listening to a song

2 What was the author's main aim when writing the passage?
- Ⓐ   To make readers agree with an opinion
- Ⓑ   To give facts and details about a person's life
- Ⓒ   To describe key events in his own life
- Ⓓ   To teach readers how to create music

3 If the passage were given another title, which title would best fit?
- Ⓐ   The Life of a Great Composer
- Ⓑ   How to Compose Music
- Ⓒ   Living in Austria
- Ⓓ   Learn the Piano Today

4 Which sentence best shows that Mozart had a natural gift for music?
- Ⓐ   *Mozart is a famous German composer of the classical era.*
- Ⓑ   *He is also known as Wolfgang Amadeus Mozart.*
- Ⓒ   *Mozart began composing at the age of just 5.*
- Ⓓ   *Mozart wrote most of his best-known work while living in Vienna.*

Presidents

In 1789, George Washington became the first president of the United States of America. Most people know that George Washington was the first president. It is less known that John Adams was the vice president. John Adams went on to become the second president in 1797. Thomas Jefferson was his vice president. When John Adams was no longer president in 1801, Thomas Jefferson became the third president of the United States of America.

The trend of first being vice president has continued. Theodore Roosevelt, Calvin Coolidge, Harry S. Truman, Lyndon B. Johnson, Richard Nixon, Gerald Ford, and George Bush Senior were all vice presidents before they became president.

The First Five Presidents

President	Term as President
George Washington	1789 to 1797
John Adams	1797 to 1801
Thomas Jefferson	1801 to 1809
James Madison	1809 to 1817
James Monroe	1817 to 1825

CORE SKILLS PRACTICE

The passage describes how some presidents were first vice presidents. Explain how you think being vice president first might benefit a president.

_____

_____

_____

_____

1   How is the first paragraph organized?
    Ⓐ   A solution to a problem is described.
    Ⓑ   Events are described in the order they occurred.
    Ⓒ   Facts are given to support an argument.
    Ⓓ   An event in the past is compared to an event today.

2   Who was president for the shortest amount of time? Tick the box to show your answer.

    ☐   George Washington   ☐   John Adams

    ☐   Thomas Jefferson   ☐   James Madison

    ☐   James Monroe

3   What is similar about John Adams and Thomas Jefferson?
    Ⓐ   They were both vice president before they became president.
    Ⓑ   They were both vice president when George Washington was president.
    Ⓒ   They were both president for 8 years or more.
    Ⓓ   They were both presidents before George Washington.

4   Which statement would the author most likely agree with?
    Ⓐ   Vice presidents are not as well known as presidents.
    Ⓑ   George Washington was the greatest president.
    Ⓒ   It is important to know the history of the United States.
    Ⓓ   Presidents need the support of those around them.

Neil Armstrong

Neil Armstrong was the first man to walk on the Moon. He did this in 1969 when he was 38 years old. The NASA space mission he went on was called Apollo 11. It was during this mission that he said the very well-known sentence, "One small step for man, one giant leap for mankind." He said this as he was stepping onto the Moon's surface.

People across America and all over the world watched the historical event live. The name Neil Armstrong became known worldwide. He has since been in newspapers and magazines. He has been on television, and movies have been made about him. He has even been put onto postage stamps. He worked hard and did something great. He is a great role model for people everywhere.

CORE SKILLS PRACTICE

The passage describes how Neil Armstrong said the famous words below as he stepped onto the Moon's surface. Explain what the statement means.

"One small step for man, one giant leap for mankind."

_____

_____

_____

_____

_____

_____

1   How would this passage most likely be different if it were an autobiography?

   Ⓐ   It would contain more facts and fewer opinions.

   Ⓑ   It would include quotes from other people.

   Ⓒ   It would provide more background about the Apollo missions.

   Ⓓ   It would show how Neil Armstrong felt about the events.

2   Which sentence from the passage gives the author's opinion?

   Ⓐ   *Neil Armstrong was the first man to walk on the Moon.*

   Ⓑ   *He did this in 1969 when he was 38 years old.*

   Ⓒ   *The NASA space mission he went on was called Apollo 11.*

   Ⓓ   *He is a great role model for people everywhere.*

3   The passage was probably written mainly to –

   Ⓐ   encourage people to become astronauts

   Ⓑ   describe the life of Neil Armstrong

   Ⓒ   tell an entertaining story

   Ⓓ   inform readers about the Moon

4   What is the main purpose of the second paragraph?

   Ⓐ   To explain why Armstrong was chosen for the mission

   Ⓑ   To tell how Armstrong became famous after the mission

   Ⓒ   To describe how Armstrong affected people's view of the Moon

   Ⓓ   To show how Armstrong inspired young people

Crying Over Onions

It is a well-known fact that chopping onions makes people cry. But why does this happen? What is the purpose of this?

It's not because onions make people sad! It is due to a gas that is released when the onion skin is cut. If the gas gets into your eyes, it causes them to sting. Your body makes you cry to help clean the gas from your eyes and stop them from stinging. This is one way that the body can help care for itself.

One way to stop your eyes from stinging is to put onions in the freezer for a while before you cut them. The cold onions will not release as much gas and so your eyes will not sting as much. Some people wear goggles to stop any fumes from getting in their eyes. In fact, you can even buy special onion goggles, though any goggles that fit firmly over your eyes will work. Another easy trick is to cut onions under an open window. The onion fumes will blow out the window instead of hanging in the air.

CORE SKILLS PRACTICE

In this passage, the author asks questions in the first paragraph. Explain why you think the author asks questions. How do the questions affect the reader?

_____

_____

_____

_____

_____

_____

1   Which word could best be used in place of chopping?

   It is a well-known fact that chopping onions makes people cry.

   Ⓐ   Eating

   Ⓑ   Cutting

   Ⓒ   Cleaning

   Ⓓ   Seeing

2   How is the second sentence below related to the first sentence?

   One way to stop your eyes from stinging is to put onions in the freezer for a while before you cut them. The cold onions will not release as much gas and so your eyes will not sting as much.

   Ⓐ   It gives a differing opinion about the claim made in the first sentence.

   Ⓑ   It gives the effect to support the advice given in the first sentence.

   Ⓒ   It gives a solution to the problem described in the first sentence.

   Ⓓ   It gives a problem caused by the actions described in the first sentence.

3   Complete the web below by listing **three** ways to prevent crying.

   How to Prevent Crying from Onions

4 Why do onions make people cry? Do you think it is a good thing or a bad thing? Use information from the passage to support your answer.

Reading Comprehension

Set 3

Literary and Informational Texts

Instructions

Read each passage. Complete the exercise under each passage.

Then complete the questions following each passage. For each multiple-choice question, fill in the circle for the correct answer. For other types of questions, follow the instructions given. Some of the questions require a written answer. Write your answer on the lines provided.

Henry the Parrot

My pet is a parrot named Henry. He enjoys eating seeds and drinking water. Henry usually behaves well and is very easy to take care of. You don't have to walk him like you would a dog, or pat him like you would a cat. All I have to do is fill his water each morning and clean his cage once a week.

My mother feeds Henry for me each day. Every time she feeds him, he gets excited and flaps his wings. One day, he was so excited that he spilled his water all over the floor! Then he stomped around in it. It was very amusing until I had to clean up the mess. I didn't really mind though. I was just happy to see Henry having such fun.

CORE SKILLS PRACTICE

This story is written from the point of view of the owner of the parrot. Imagine how the story would be different if it were told by the mother. Write a paragraph or two describing how the water was spilled. Describe the events from the point of view of the mother.

_____

_____

_____

_____

_____

_____

_____

1 According to the passage, why does Henry flap his wings?

- Ⓐ Because he is hungry
- Ⓑ Because he is excited
- Ⓒ Because he is annoyed
- Ⓓ Because he is thirsty

2 According to the passage, what does Henry eat?

- Ⓐ Worms
- Ⓑ Crumbs
- Ⓒ Bugs
- Ⓓ Seeds

3 In the sentence below, which word means the same as <u>amusing</u>?

It was very amusing until I had to clean up the mess.

- Ⓐ Annoying
- Ⓑ Noisy
- Ⓒ Weird
- Ⓓ Funny

4 Why does the author compare Henry to a cat and a dog?

- Ⓐ To explain how to take care of a parrot
- Ⓑ To show that Henry is easy to look after
- Ⓒ To warn that parrots are not exciting pets
- Ⓓ To suggest that Henry is not her only pet

An Unusual Gift

Alexander Graham Bell was the man who invented the telephone. He was born in Scotland in 1847. When Bell was born, he was not given a middle name. He disliked not having one and begged his father for one. His two brothers both had one, and he wanted one as well.

Alexander Bell was 11 years old when he got a middle name. The middle name of "Graham" was given to him from his father as a gift for his 11th birthday. The name was chosen to honor a close family friend named Alexander Graham. Many kids his age would have been begging for a bike, so Alexander's birthday gift was unusual. However, it was a gift he kept and treasured for the rest of his life.

CORE SKILLS PRACTICE

This passage contains many facts about Alexander Graham Bell. Facts are details that can be proven to be true. Complete the list of facts by adding **four** more facts to the list.

Facts about Alexander Graham Bell

1. He was born in Scotland.

2. _____

3. _____

4. _____

5. _____

1. What is the passage mostly about?
   - Ⓐ How Alexander Graham Bell invented the telephone
   - Ⓑ Alexander Graham Bell's middle name
   - Ⓒ Common birthday presents given to children
   - Ⓓ Why "Graham" was chosen as a middle name

2. Why does the author say that Bell "treasured" his middle name in the last sentence?
   - Ⓐ To show that it was important to him
   - Ⓑ To show that he kept it a secret
   - Ⓒ To show that he felt bad about asking for it
   - Ⓓ To show that it helped to make him famous

3. What is the main purpose of the passage?
   - Ⓐ To instruct people on how to choose a middle name
   - Ⓑ To entertain readers with an amusing story
   - Ⓒ To persuade readers to give special presents
   - Ⓓ To inform readers of an interesting fact

4. Which sentence shows how badly Bell wanted a middle name?
   - Ⓐ *When Bell was born, he was not given a middle name.*
   - Ⓑ *He disliked not having one and begged his father for one.*
   - Ⓒ *Alexander Bell was 11 years old when he got a middle name.*
   - Ⓓ *The name was chosen to honor a close family friend named Alexander Graham.*

Soil

Soil is necessary to grow most plants. It contains the materials that a plant needs to grow. This includes the water and minerals that plants need. Some places, such as deserts, may have soil that does not contain everything that a plant needs. This means that plants are not as likely to live there.

Good soil usually feels moist, but not soaking wet. It is commonly a dark brown color. This is due to all of the animals and plants living in it. The animals keep the soil moving and add food to the soil.

Worms are especially important for healthy soil. They break down dead plant matter, which makes minerals available to growing plants. They make the soil softer, which helps the roots of plants move deeper into the soil. Their burrows also act a bit like the holes in sponges and help water drain from the soil.

CORE SKILLS PRACTICE

Look at the photograph. What ideas in the passage does the photograph support? Explain your answer.

_____

_____

_____

_____

_____

_____

1 Which word could best be used in place of moist?

Good soil usually feels moist, but not soaking wet.

- Ⓐ Cold
- Ⓑ Damp
- Ⓒ Clean
- Ⓓ Fine

2 Which word would NOT be used to describe good soil?
- Ⓐ Moist
- Ⓑ Brown
- Ⓒ Dark
- Ⓓ Dry

3 What is the second paragraph mostly about?
- Ⓐ What plants need to grow
- Ⓑ How few plants grow in deserts
- Ⓒ Why plants need soil
- Ⓓ What good soil is like

4 Complete the web below by listing **two** more ways that worms help soil.

```
          How Worms Help Create Healthy Soil
         /              |               \
  They make
  minerals
  available to
  plants.
```

Stewart the Dragon

Stewart was a very big green dragon. He lived in a cave on the top of a hill. The people in the town below were very scared of him. If they ever saw Stewart, they ran inside to hide. This made Stewart very sad. He did not want to hurt anybody. He just wanted to be part of the town. It always looked like everyone was having lots of fun. Unfortunately, whenever Stewart opened his mouth to say hello, flames poured out. He was just trying to be friendly, but everyone screamed as soon as they saw the flames and raced away.

One night it was very cold, and the people of the town could not start a fire. Stewart went down to the town. He breathed gently on the fire and it roared to life. The people of the town realized that Stewart was a kind dragon. They invited Stewart to come down to the town every night. Stewart started the fire each night. Then he dined with the villagers, before returning happily to his home.

CORE SKILLS PRACTICE

The theme of a story is the message of a story, or what can be learned from it. What is the theme of this story? Explain how the story gets its message across.

_____

_____

_____

_____

_____

_____

1 Where does Stewart the Dragon live?

- Ⓐ In a forest
- Ⓑ In a village
- Ⓒ In a cave
- Ⓓ In a swamp

2 What is the second paragraph mainly about?

- Ⓐ Why the people of the town are scared of Stewart
- Ⓑ How Stewart becomes part of the town
- Ⓒ What Stewart and the people of the town eat
- Ⓓ How the people were tricked by Stewart

3 Which word best describes Stewart in the first paragraph?

- Ⓐ Lonely
- Ⓑ Angry
- Ⓒ Patient
- Ⓓ Kind

4 Which sentence explains why the people not being able to light the fire is important to the plot?

- Ⓐ It stopped everyone from running inside to hide.
- Ⓑ It allowed Stewart to sneak down to the village.
- Ⓒ It made the people feel sad like Stewart.
- Ⓓ It gave Stewart a chance to help the people.

5 How do the people of the town feel about Stewart at the start of the passage? How do their feelings change in the passage? Use information from the passage to support your answer.

Reading Comprehension

Set 4

Literary and Informational Texts

Instructions

Read each passage. Complete the exercise under each passage.

Then complete the questions following each passage. For each multiple-choice question, fill in the circle for the correct answer. For other types of questions, follow the instructions given. Some of the questions require a written answer. Write your answer on the lines provided.

A Letter to Grandma

Dear Grandma,

Today my school held a school fair. It was held on the football fields. There were stalls and rides to help raise money for building a school hall. I went on a lot of rides! One ride spun me around and around faster and faster. I felt like a spinning top. I played a dart game where I had to throw a dart to pop a balloon. I popped a red balloon and won a key ring. I gave the key ring to Mom.

There was also a lady who was painting faces. I could not decide on what I wanted her to paint on me. I finally decided on a cat. Dad was so silly. He thought I was a tiger! Why would I want to be a tiger? Before we left, I bought some choc chip cookies. They tasted great.

Love,

Anna

CORE SKILLS PRACTICE

This passage contains many details. Locate the detail that answers each question below.

Where was the school fair held? _____

What did Anna win? _____

What did Anna get her face painted as? _____

What did Anna buy? _____

1 Why does Anna say she "felt like a spinning top"?

- Ⓐ To show that the rides made her sick
- Ⓑ To show that she had a lot of fun
- Ⓒ To show that she spun very fast
- Ⓓ To show that she went high in the air

2 Which word would Anna most likely use to describe the school fair?

- Ⓐ Fun
- Ⓑ Stressful
- Ⓒ Scary
- Ⓓ Relaxing

3 The school fair was held to raise money for –

- Ⓐ buying new computers
- Ⓑ adding a school library
- Ⓒ fixing the football field
- Ⓓ building a school hall

4 Complete the chart by listing **four** things Anna did at the school fair.

```
┌──────────┐                      ┌──────────┐
│          │                      │          │
└────────┐ │                      │ ┌────────┘
         │ │   ┌──────────────┐   │ │
         └─┼───┤ What Anna Did├───┼─┘
         ┌─┼───┤at the School │───┼─┐
         │ │   │     Fair     │   │ │
┌────────┘ │   └──────────────┘   │ └────────┐
│          │                      │          │
└──────────┘                      └──────────┘
```

Sound

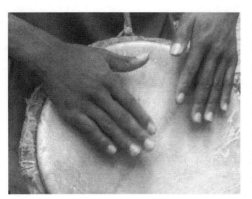

A drummer beats on a drum. You can hear the sound of the beating drum. But how does the sound travel from the drum to your ears? Sound is caused by vibrations moving through the air. The skin of the drum vibrates. This causes the air to vibrate. The vibrations move through the air. When it reaches our ears, the vibrations are picked up by our ear drums.

When a sound is made in water, the vibrations travel faster than when they are in air. The sound travels about four times faster in water.

People use sound all the time to talk to each other. Animals also use sound to "talk" to each other. Adult animals use sounds to communicate with their young. Birds can sing to attract a mate. Animals can make loud noises to scare other animals away. Sound can be used to warn others of danger. A bird might call out to tell other birds that there is a fox nearby.

CORE SKILLS PRACTICE

This passage has three paragraphs. Each paragraph has a different topic. Describe the topic of each paragraph. The topic of the first paragraph has been completed for you.

Paragraph 1: How sound is caused by vibrations

Paragraph 2: _____

_____

Paragraph 3: _____

_____

1 Read this sentence from the passage.

> **A bird might call out to tell other birds that there is a fox nearby.**

What is this sentence used as an example of?
- Ⓐ An animal making sounds to attract a mate
- Ⓑ An animal making sounds to scare another animal away
- Ⓒ An animal making sounds to warn other animals of danger
- Ⓓ An animal making sounds to communicate with the young

2 According to the passage, sounds made in water –
- Ⓐ are louder than sounds made in air
- Ⓑ are softer than sounds made in air
- Ⓒ travel faster than sounds made in air
- Ⓓ travel slower than sounds made in air

3 How is the first paragraph mainly organized?
- Ⓐ A solution to a problem is described.
- Ⓑ A question is asked and then answered.
- Ⓒ Facts are given to support an argument.
- Ⓓ Two different sounds are compared.

4 Which sentence from the passage compares two things?
- Ⓐ *You can hear the sound of the beating drum.*
- Ⓑ *This causes the air to vibrate.*
- Ⓒ *The sound travels about four times faster in water.*
- Ⓓ *People use sound all the time to talk to each other.*

A Fresh Coat of Paint

Dad decided to paint my bedroom walls. I wanted them to be blue like the sea. Mom wanted to paint them yellow like the Sun. She said it would be brighter. I thought it would be too bright. I wanted my room to be a cheerful place, but also a place I could relax in.

Dad decided that we should mix the two colors together. We took the yellow paint and the blue paint. We poured them both into a bucket. After mixing the paint, I saw a pretty light green color. I nodded as soon as I saw it and then Dad got to work painting. It makes me think of freshly mowed grass in summer. I can lie back reading a book and it's almost like I'm lying in a meadow. It's pretty and peaceful and I couldn't have asked for anything more perfect.

CORE SKILLS PRACTICE

Think about the problem in the story and how it is solved. Then give your opinion by answering the question below.

Do you think the father's solution to the problem is a good one? Explain why or why not.

_____

_____

_____

_____

_____

_____

1. What is the main problem in the passage?
    - Ⓐ They do not mix the paint properly.
    - Ⓑ They do not know how to paint a bedroom.
    - Ⓒ They cannot decide what color to paint the bedroom.
    - Ⓓ They cannot find enough yellow or blue paint.

2. What color does the bedroom get painted?
    - Ⓐ Yellow
    - Ⓑ Blue
    - Ⓒ Green
    - Ⓓ Red

3. How does the narrator feel about her painted bedroom?
    - Ⓐ Pleased
    - Ⓑ Annoyed
    - Ⓒ Confused
    - Ⓓ Worried

4. The narrator describes how she can "lie back reading a book and it's almost like I'm lying in a meadow." What does this detail best show?
    - Ⓐ That she is glad that she didn't have to do any of the painting
    - Ⓑ That she finds her room a relaxing place like she wanted
    - Ⓒ That the walls have blue and yellow colors in them
    - Ⓓ That it wouldn't really have mattered what color the walls were

Deviled Eggs

Deviled eggs are a yummy treat to make and eat. They are quick and easy to make too! To make deviled eggs you will need:

- hard boiled eggs (Warning: make sure you let them cool first.)
- ¼ cup of mayonnaise
- ½ teaspoon of mustard
- ½ teaspoon of white vinegar

What to Do

1. Take off the shells of the boiled eggs and cut the eggs in half.
2. Take out the yolk and place it in a bowl.
3. Mix the other ingredients with the yolk and mash it up with a fork.
4. Using a spoon, put the yolk mix back in the holes of the hard boiled eggs.

You can sprinkle them with herbs like parsley or chives to make them look even nicer. Yum! Your tasty snack is ready to eat.

CORE SKILLS PRACTICE

Think of a simple snack or meal that you have made. Describe how you made that snack or meal.

_____

_____

_____

_____

_____

1 Which words does the author use to show readers that the deviled eggs will taste good?

- Ⓐ *yummy treat*
- Ⓑ *make and eat*
- Ⓒ *quick and easy*
- Ⓓ *hard boiled eggs*

2 What is the main purpose of the passage?

- Ⓐ To teach readers how to do something
- Ⓑ To entertain readers with a story
- Ⓒ To inform readers about eggs
- Ⓓ To make readers want to eat more eggs

3 In which step of the directions is a fork needed?

- Ⓐ Step 1
- Ⓑ Step 2
- Ⓒ Step 3
- Ⓓ Step 4

4 What is the most likely reason it is important to let the hard boiled eggs cool?

- Ⓐ So the eggs are easy to cut in half
- Ⓑ So the yolk has time to harden
- Ⓒ So the deviled eggs taste better
- Ⓓ So you do not burn your hands when you take off the shells

5 Do you think that deviled eggs would be easy to make? Use information from the passage to support your answer.

Reading Comprehension

Set 5

Paired Literary Texts

Instructions

This set contains a pair of passages. Read each passage on its own first. Complete the exercise under each passage. Then complete the questions following each passage.

For each multiple-choice question, fill in the circle for the correct answer. For other types of questions, follow the instructions given. Some of the questions require a written answer. Write your answer on the lines provided.

After reading both passages, you will answer one or more additional questions. You will use information from both passages to answer these questions. Write your answers on the lines provided.

Bread and Milk

Niral's mother asked her to go to the store to buy some bread and milk. She gave her five dollars. When Niral got to the store, she found that the bread and milk cost almost six dollars. She knew that she needed one more dollar. She didn't want to walk all the way home without the bread and milk. She looked so lost that the shopkeeper asked her what was wrong. She explained her problem to him.

"Don't worry," the shopkeeper said. "You can have both items for five dollars today for being such a good customer!"

Niral walked home happily. She told her mother of her adventure.

CORE SKILLS PRACTICE

A summary is a description of the events of a story. A summary should include only the main events from the story. Write a summary of the story "Bread and Milk."

_____

_____

_____

_____

_____

_____

_____

Reading Comprehension, Common Core Workbook, Grade 3

1 Read this sentence from the passage.

> **She looked so lost that the shopkeeper asked her what was wrong.**

Why did Niral most likely look lost?
- Ⓐ   She didn't know what to do.
- Ⓑ   She didn't know where she was.
- Ⓒ   She couldn't find the bread and milk.
- Ⓓ   She didn't know the way home.

2 What is Niral's main problem in the passage?
- Ⓐ   She does not have enough money for the bread and milk.
- Ⓑ   She has to go to the store to buy bread and milk.
- Ⓒ   The shopkeeper lets her buy bread and milk for five dollars.
- Ⓓ   The shop is too far from her home.

3 Which word best describes the shopkeeper?
- Ⓐ   Smart
- Ⓑ   Rude
- Ⓒ   Kind
- Ⓓ   Funny

4 How does Niral most likely feel when the shopkeeper says she can have both items for five dollars?
- Ⓐ   Greedy
- Ⓑ   Shocked
- Ⓒ   Puzzled
- Ⓓ   Thankful

Missing

James was wandering around the classroom looking very frazzled. He was pushing chairs aside and poking around under desks and lifting up boxes and bins. When Sarah asked him what was wrong, he told her that he had lost his USB drive. It had an essay on it he had written in class for an assignment. The essay on it was due tomorrow and he needed to take it home and finish it off. He knew it must be around somewhere and he refused to go home without it.

Sarah helped James look for the missing drive. After a few minutes, Sarah held up a USB drive and cried out that she'd found it. James was relieved at first, but then disappointed when he saw that it was red. The one that James lost was black. Sarah told James not to worry and that they would keep looking until they found it. James was glad he had a friend to help him search. They finally found the drive under the teacher's desk. James tucked it carefully in his pocket and thanked Sarah for her help.

CORE SKILLS PRACTICE

You can tell a lot about characters by what they do. How do the actions of James show that he is very keen to find the USB drive?

_____

_____

_____

_____

_____

5 In the sentence below, the word <u>frazzled</u> shows that James is —

   James was wandering around the classroom looking very frazzled.

   Ⓐ upset
   Ⓑ determined
   Ⓒ calm
   Ⓓ excited

6 What color was the USB drive that James lost?
   Ⓐ Green
   Ⓑ White
   Ⓒ Black
   Ⓓ Red

7 What happens right after James tells Sarah that he has lost his USB drive?
   Ⓐ They look for the drive.
   Ⓑ They find a red drive.
   Ⓒ James writes an essay.
   Ⓓ Sarah tells James not to worry.

8 Which sentence best tells why it is important that James finds the drive?
   Ⓐ *James was wandering around the classroom looking very frazzled.*
   Ⓑ *When Sarah asked him what was wrong, he told her that he had lost his USB drive.*
   Ⓒ *The essay on it was due tomorrow and he needed to take it home and finish it off.*
   Ⓓ *After a few minutes, Sarah held up a USB drive and cried out that she'd found it.*

Directions: Use both passages to answer the following questions.

9 How are the shopkeeper in "Bread and Milk" and Sarah in "Missing" similar? Explain your answer.

_____

_____

_____

_____

_____

10 Describe the problems that James and Niral have. Who do you think has the most serious problem? Explain your answer.

_____

_____

_____

_____

_____

Reading Comprehension

Set 6

Paired Informational Texts

Instructions

This set contains a pair of passages. Read each passage on its own first. Complete the exercise under each passage. Then complete the questions following each passage.

For each multiple-choice question, fill in the circle for the correct answer. For other types of questions, follow the instructions given. Some of the questions require a written answer. Write your answer on the lines provided.

After reading both passages, you will answer one or more additional questions. You will use information from both passages to answer these questions. Write your answers on the lines provided.

Jupiter

Jupiter is the fifth planet from the Sun and the largest planet in the Solar System. Jupiter is made up of gases. It does not have a hard crust like the Earth does. This means that there is no solid place for a spaceship or rocket to land. This makes it hard for scientists to study Jupiter. But scientists have found a way.

Scientists have sent unmanned spacecraft to study Jupiter. The *Galileo* spacecraft was launched in 1989 and arrived at Jupiter in 1995. It was in orbit around Jupiter for 8 years. While it was circling the planet, it collected data and took photos. It gave scientists a new understanding of Jupiter and its 16 moons.

Another spacecraft named *Juno* was launched in August, 2011. It will arrive at Jupiter in July, 2016. It is expected to orbit Jupiter 33 times over a period of just over a year. Its advanced equipment will collect data and provide even more information about Jupiter.

CORE SKILLS PRACTICE

You will often be asked to describe how two things are different. This is known as contrasting. Complete the table to summarize how Jupiter is different from Earth.

Feature	Earth	Jupiter
Distance from the Sun	Third planet from the Sun	
Number of Moons	1	
Surface	Hard crust	

1. Which word in the second paragraph helps the reader know what <u>orbit</u> means?
   - Ⓐ *unmanned*
   - Ⓑ *launched*
   - Ⓒ *circling*
   - Ⓓ *photos*

2. What is the second paragraph mostly about?
   - Ⓐ What scientists have learned about Jupiter
   - Ⓑ How scientists study Jupiter
   - Ⓒ Why it is hard to study Jupiter
   - Ⓓ What Jupiter looks like

3. Why is a spaceship unable to land on Jupiter?
   - Ⓐ It has too many moons.
   - Ⓑ It is too far away.
   - Ⓒ It is too large.
   - Ⓓ It is made up of gases.

4. What does the photograph in the passage represent?
   - Ⓐ How far Jupiter is from Earth
   - Ⓑ Why Jupiter is difficult to study
   - Ⓒ How many moons Jupiter has
   - Ⓓ How spacecrafts study Jupiter

Poor Pluto

Until 2006, Pluto was the ninth planet in our Solar System. It is still there, but it was renamed. It is no longer known as a planet because Pluto was changed to a dwarf planet. This change occurred because of its size. This means that while it is not a star or moon, it is not big enough to be a planet.

Pluto is farther from the Sun than all of the other planets in the Solar System. The makes the temperature on Pluto very low. A lot is still not known about Pluto because it so far from Earth. However, more will be known when a space probe named *New Horizons* flies by in July of 2015. It's been a long wait for that information. The space probe left Earth in January, 2006.

Pluto is about 5 times smaller than Earth and is even smaller than Earth's Moon.

CORE SKILLS PRACTICE

Describe **two** ways that Pluto is different from the planets of the Solar System.

1. _____

_____

2. _____

_____

5   What does the title of the passage suggest about Pluto?
   Ⓐ   It is sad that Pluto is no longer a planet.
   Ⓑ   Pluto is a cold and icy planet.
   Ⓒ   Pluto is too far away to be visited.
   Ⓓ   Pluto's name should be changed.

6   Why was Pluto changed to a dwarf planet?
   Ⓐ   It is too far away.
   Ⓑ   It is too cold.
   Ⓒ   It is too small.
   Ⓓ   It is too rocky.

7   What is the main purpose of the passage?
   Ⓐ   To instruct
   Ⓑ   To entertain
   Ⓒ   To persuade
   Ⓓ   To inform

8   What does the illustration mainly help readers understand?
   Ⓐ   How long it takes to reach Pluto from Earth
   Ⓑ   How little is known about what Pluto is like
   Ⓒ   How small Pluto is compared to planets
   Ⓓ   How low the temperature is on Pluto

Directions: Use both passages to answer the following questions.

9   Scientists still do not know everything about Jupiter, and know even less about Pluto. Explain why it is difficult to learn about Jupiter and Pluto. Use information from both passages to support your answer.

_____

_____

_____

_____

_____

10   Why do scientists studying the planets need to be very patient? Use information from both passages to support your answer.

_____

_____

_____

_____

_____

Reading Comprehension

Set 7

Literary Texts

Instructions

Read each passage. Complete the exercise under each passage.

Then complete the questions following each passage. For each multiple-choice question, fill in the circle for the correct answer. For other types of questions, follow the instructions given. Some of the questions require a written answer. Write your answer on the lines provided.

Animal Noises

I have a problem.
It's difficult you see.
Animal noises
are just not for me!

I tried and I tried
to bark like a dog.
Mother said,
"Timmy, you sound like a squashed frog!"

I didn't want to give up,
so I tried growling.
Mother said,
"Timmy, you sound like a sick wolf howling."

CORE SKILLS PRACTICE

Authors write poems for different purposes. Some poems are meant to be serious. Others are meant to be funny. Do you think this poem is meant to be serious or funny? Explain your answer.

_____
_____
_____
_____
_____
_____
_____

1. The art with the poem helps make the poem seem –
   - Ⓐ sad
   - Ⓑ angry
   - Ⓒ playful
   - Ⓓ gloomy

2. What is the rhyme pattern of each stanza of the poem?
   - Ⓐ Every line rhymes.
   - Ⓑ The second and fourth lines rhyme.
   - Ⓒ The first and last lines rhyme.
   - Ⓓ The first and third lines rhyme.

3. Read these lines from the poem.

   **I tried and I tried
   to bark like a dog.**

   Why does the author most likely repeat "I tried" in these lines?
   - Ⓐ To show that he tried hard
   - Ⓑ To show that he should not have tried
   - Ⓒ To show that he could not bark
   - Ⓓ To show what he sounded like

4. What does the mother's dialogue in the poem reveal?
   - Ⓐ That Timmy is getting ill
   - Ⓑ That Timmy's noises sound terrible
   - Ⓒ That Timmy is not being loud enough
   - Ⓓ The Timmy finds making animal noises funny

My Duck Family

I am a duck. I go by the name of Frankie. I live in a pond, in a park, with many other ducks. I have three ducklings named Fuzzy, Feathers, and Fergie. We enjoy swimming around the pond. We love eating bread that the kind humans throw to us. Bread tastes mighty yummy. Catching the bread first is a fun game to play with my duck family! We sometimes flap our wings wildly or dive at each other. It might look like we're all mad at each other, but we're really just having fun. There are lots of humans that feed us, so we never go hungry.

CORE SKILLS PRACTICE

This story is told from the point of view of a duck. The speaker in the story is a duck. Think of another animal. Write a paragraph about something the animal enjoys. Make sure you write from the point of view of the animal.

_____

_____

_____

_____

_____

_____

_____

_____

1 Which word means the opposite of kind?

We love eating bread that the kind humans throw to us.

- Ⓐ Mean
- Ⓑ Grumpy
- Ⓒ Sad
- Ⓓ Nice

2 Who is telling the story?
- Ⓐ Frankie
- Ⓑ Fuzzy
- Ⓒ Feathers
- Ⓓ Fergie

3 Where does the duck family live?
- Ⓐ In a forest
- Ⓑ In a backyard
- Ⓒ In a park
- Ⓓ In a zoo

4 According to the passage, why do the ducks fight over the bread?
- Ⓐ They are trying to scare away other ducks.
- Ⓑ They are enjoying playing a game.
- Ⓒ They are showing off for the humans.
- Ⓓ They are trying to get enough for their families.

Sports Day

Today is the day my class plays sport. Our teacher asked us which sport we wanted to play. I said I wanted to play football the most. My friend Ling said he wanted to play baseball. It seemed like everyone had different ideas.

The teacher asked everyone in the class to choose between football, baseball, basketball, and hockey. The teacher added up how many votes there were for each sport. We ended up playing basketball. Our teacher said that it was only fair that we played basketball.

CORE SKILLS PRACTICE

Sometimes you will be asked to give your opinion about something. This means that you will write about what you think. Give your opinion by answering the question below.

Do you think the way the teacher chose the sport was fair? Explain your answer.

_____

_____

_____

_____

_____

_____

1 Which meaning of the word <u>fair</u> is used in the sentence below?

Our teacher said that it was only fair that we played basketball.

- Ⓐ Pale or light
- Ⓑ Right or just
- Ⓒ Fine or clear
- Ⓓ Circus or carnival

2 Which sport does Ling most want to play?
- Ⓐ Football
- Ⓑ Baseball
- Ⓒ Basketball
- Ⓓ Hockey

3 Which conclusion can best be drawn from the passage?
- Ⓐ Basketball had the most votes.
- Ⓑ Basketball had the least votes.
- Ⓒ Basketball was the teacher's favorite sport.
- Ⓓ Basketball was the teacher's least favorite sport.

4 What is the main purpose of the first paragraph?
- Ⓐ It introduces the main problem.
- Ⓑ It gives the main character's opinion.
- Ⓒ It tells how a problem is solved.
- Ⓓ It states the lesson the passage teaches.

To the Moon

Dear Alexa,

I have decided that when I grow up I want to be an astronaut. They go up into space! I want to bounce around on the Moon like Neil Armstrong. He was the first person to walk on the Moon. I am not sure if there are any monsters in space. If there are any, I am sure they would be friendly. How could they be angry? They live in space. How cool is that?

Bye for now,

Jin

CORE SKILLS PRACTICE

In a study completed in 2013, 9 out of 100 third grade students chose being an astronaut as the career they would most like to have. What do you think makes being an astronaut such a popular choice?

_____

_____

_____

_____

_____

_____

1 The word <u>bounce</u> suggests that moving on the Moon would be –

   I want to bounce around on the Moon like Neil Armstrong.

   Ⓐ difficult

   Ⓑ enjoyable

   Ⓒ simple

   Ⓓ dangerous

2 Which word would Jin most likely use to describe being an astronaut?

   Ⓐ Scary

   Ⓑ Fun

   Ⓒ Difficult

   Ⓓ Strange

3 What type of passage is "To the Moon"?

   Ⓐ Short story

   Ⓑ Science fiction story

   Ⓒ Letter

   Ⓓ Fable

4 Based on your answer to Question 3, which feature of the passage is common to the passage type?

   Ⓐ It has a turning point.

   Ⓑ It is set in space.

   Ⓒ It is written in first-person.

   Ⓓ It has a lesson to be learned.

5 Jin writes that she wants to be an astronaut. Do you think that Jin is serious about this goal? Use details from the passage to support your answer.

Reading Comprehension

Set 8

Informational Texts

Instructions

Read each passage. Complete the exercise under each passage.

Then complete the questions following each passage. For each multiple-choice question, fill in the circle for the correct answer. For other types of questions, follow the instructions given. Some of the questions require a written answer. Write your answer on the lines provided.

Stingrays

Stingrays are a type of fish. They are related to sharks, but they look very different. They have a long flat body. They have large flat fins that look more like giant wings. They move the fins up and down to help them glide through the water. They are named for the stinger on their tail.

Stingrays mainly live in coastal waters. They can be found in rivers, estuaries, and at beaches. Stingrays are not aggressive animals and will not attack people on purpose. Most injuries occur when people accidentally step on a stingray. In shallow waters, stingrays often hide under a thin layer of sand. This makes them hard to spot and can cause people to step on one without ever knowing it was there. In places where people know there are stingrays, they throw small stones into the water before walking through. Another way to avoid stingrays is to shuffle through the water. Stingrays will feel the sand move and swim away.

CORE SKILLS PRACTICE

Many passages include pictures or photographs. These can help the reader understand information in the passage. Describe two things the photograph in the passage helps you understand.

_____

_____

_____

_____

_____

1. What is the main way that sharks and stingrays are similar?
   - Ⓐ They are types of fish.
   - Ⓑ They have stingers.
   - Ⓒ They hide under sand.
   - Ⓓ They have fins like wings.

2. Why do people most likely throw stones into the water?
   - Ⓐ To scare away the stingrays
   - Ⓑ To harm the stingrays
   - Ⓒ To amuse the stingrays
   - Ⓓ To attracts sharks to the stingrays

3. Which detail from the passage best shows that stingrays can harm people?
   - Ⓐ They live in the sea.
   - Ⓑ They are related to sharks.
   - Ⓒ They have stingers on their tails.
   - Ⓓ They have large flat fins.

4. Which detail best explains why people sometimes step on stingrays?
   - Ⓐ Stingrays glide through the water.
   - Ⓑ Stingrays live in coastal waters.
   - Ⓒ Stingrays are not aggressive animals.
   - Ⓓ Stingrays hide under a layer of sand.

Basketball

Basketball is a game that has ten players divided into two teams. This means that each team has five players. To play basketball, you bounce a ball and score points by throwing the ball into the basket.

There is a basket at the top of a post on each side of the court. Each team has a basket to keep safe from the other team. Some people play basketball for their career. Most of those players are over 6 feet tall. Even with natural talent, it takes hard work to play as a professional.

CORE SKILLS PRACTICE

Sometimes you will be asked to make inferences. This means that you must guess something based on the information given. You can also sometimes use your own knowledge. Answer the question below by making an inference.

Why do you think most people who play basketball for their career are over 6 feet tall?

_____

_____

_____

_____

_____

_____

1   Which word means about the same as <u>career</u>?

Some people play basketball for their career.

- Ⓐ   Exercise
- Ⓑ   Serious
- Ⓒ   Job
- Ⓓ   Fun

2   What is the main purpose of the passage?
- Ⓐ   To describe how a sport is played
- Ⓑ   To encourage people to play sport
- Ⓒ   To show that there are sports for everyone
- Ⓓ   To tell an interesting story about sport

3   How many players are in a basketball team? Circle the correct answer.

| 1 | 2 | 3 | 4 | 5 |
| 6 | 7 | 8 | 9 | 10 |

4   Select the sentence from the last paragraph that is an opinion.

☐   *There is a basket at the top of a post on each side of the court.*

☐   *Each team has a basket to keep safe from the other team.*

☐   *Some people play basketball for their career.*

☐   *Most of those players are over 6 feet tall.*

☐   *Even with natural talent, it takes hard work to play as a professional.*

Turtles

Turtles are the only reptiles that have shells. Turtles use their shells for protection by pulling their heads, arms, and legs inside of their shell. Most turtles live in fresh water. Like all reptiles, turtles lay eggs. If a turtle lives mostly on land, it is known as a tortoise. They look different to turtles and will often be much bigger.

Turtles can be a lot of fun to watch swim in a pond. However, you should only watch them and never try to catch them. Turtles are not dangerous, but trying to pick them up could injure them. They will be safer and happier if you leave them in their home.

CORE SKILLS PRACTICE

Describe **three** ways that tortoises are different from turtles.

1. _____

_____

2. _____

_____

3. _____

_____

1 Which sentence best shows that a turtle's shell helps it survive?

Ⓐ *Turtles are the only reptiles that have shells.*

Ⓑ *Turtles use their shells for protection by pulling their heads, arms, and legs inside of their shell.*

Ⓒ *However, you should only watch them and never try to catch them.*

Ⓓ *Turtles are not dangerous, but trying to pick them up could injure them.*

2 How are turtles different from all reptiles?

Ⓐ They have arms.

Ⓑ They have shells.

Ⓒ They have legs.

Ⓓ They lay eggs.

3 Based on the information in the passage, when would a turtle be most likely to pull its head inside its shell?

Ⓐ When it is tired

Ⓑ When it is swimming

Ⓒ When it is scared

Ⓓ When it is hungry

4 The article says that picking up turtles could <u>injure</u> them. <u>Injure</u> means –

Ⓐ scare

Ⓑ hurt

Ⓒ save

Ⓓ please

Bones

Bones are a very important part of the body. When a baby human is born, it has over 270 bones. Over time, many of the bones fuse to others to make a larger bone. Fully grown adult humans have about 206 bones. Bones are made of hard materials. The most important material is calcium.

Humans need calcium to keep their bones healthy. This is especially important when you are young and your bones are still growing. The best way to make sure you get enough calcium is by having a diet with plenty of dairy products like milk, cheese, and yogurt. Calcium is also found in green vegetables like broccoli. It is also found in shellfish, sardines, and almonds.

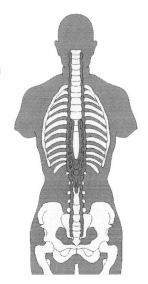

CORE SKILLS PRACTICE

Authors write passages for many reasons. They might write to entertain, to describe something, to explain something, or to teach. The main purpose of this passage is to persuade, or to get the reader to do something. Describe what the author wants the reader to do.

_____

_____

_____

_____

_____

_____

1. In the sentence below, which word means about the same as <u>fuse</u>?

   Over time, many of the bones fuse to others to make a larger bone.

   Ⓐ Move

   Ⓑ Bend

   Ⓒ Lose

   Ⓓ Join

2. Complete the web below using information from the passage.

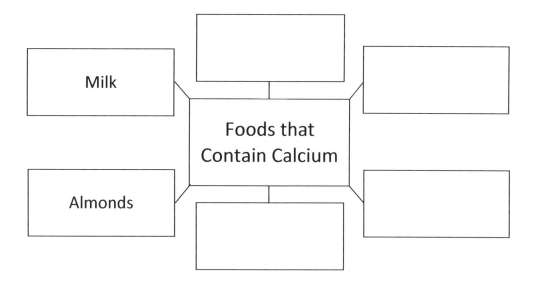

3. According to the passage, how are adults different from children?

   Ⓐ They have more bones.

   Ⓑ They have fewer bones.

   Ⓒ They have weaker bones.

   Ⓓ They have stronger bones.

4 Explain how to have healthy bones. What should you have in your diet to have healthy bones? Use details from the passage to support your answer.

Reading Comprehension

Set 9

Literary and Informational Texts

Instructions

Read each passage. Complete the exercise under each passage.

Then complete the questions following each passage. For each multiple-choice question, fill in the circle for the correct answer. For other types of questions, follow the instructions given. Some of the questions require a written answer. Write your answer on the lines provided.

Painted Eggs

Painting eggs can be a fun activity. Make sure that you ask an adult for help as eggs can break easily and cause a mess.

Step 1: Using a pin, poke small holes in the top and bottom of the egg.

Step 2: Stand over the sink and press your lips to one of the holes in the egg and blow. This will cause all the inside of the egg to leak out of the bottom hole.

Step 3: Rinse the egg with water.

Step 4: Paint the egg. You can use a paintbrush to paint the eggs. You could paint stars, flowers, or stripes onto the eggs. You can also dip the egg into different colored paints.

CORE SKILLS PRACTICE

This passage organizes the information by listing steps. Do you think this is a good way to organize the passage? Explain why or why not.

_____

_____

_____

_____

_____

_____

1. What is the most likely reason you should complete Step 2 while standing over the sink?
   - Ⓐ So you remove all the egg
   - Ⓑ So you do not make a mess
   - Ⓒ So you do not break the egg
   - Ⓓ So you do not drop the egg

2. In which step is a pin needed?
   - Ⓐ Step 1
   - Ⓑ Step 2
   - Ⓒ Step 3
   - Ⓓ Step 4

3. What does the illustration show?
   - Ⓐ What the finished eggs might look like
   - Ⓑ How to make painted eggs
   - Ⓒ How to complete the first step
   - Ⓓ Why large eggs should be used

4. In which sentence does the word <u>blow</u> mean the same as in Step 2?
   - Ⓐ Losing the match was a huge <u>blow</u> to the team.
   - Ⓑ Sam was ready to <u>blow</u> out the candles on his cake.
   - Ⓒ The campers woke up to the loud <u>blow</u> of the horn.
   - Ⓓ Graham got a <u>blow</u> to his head when he fell off his bike.

The Great Barrier Reef

The Great Barrier Reef is found off the coast of Queensland in Australia. It is the largest reef in the world. It is almost 1,500 miles long. It is actually made up of many smaller reefs and islands that follow each other in a long line just off the coast. The reef is protected. This means that there are rules for what can be done near the reef. There are many tourist businesses, but they have to follow certain rules. People can fish near the reef, but there are limits on how many fish they can take. There are many other rules as well and people monitor the reef to make sure it is not being damaged. This will help it stay healthy for many years. It is important that the reef is not lost. It is too unique and special to be lost.

The reef is very popular. A lot of people travel to the reef each year to see the coral and fish. They snorkel, scuba dive, or view the reef from glass-bottom boats. There are many beautiful and interesting fish to be seen. It has been said that the reef is one of the seven natural wonders of the world.

CORE SKILLS PRACTICE

You can often tell what a word means by how it is used. You can read the sentence the word is used in, and the sentences around it. Look for each word below in the passage. Then write a definition of each word.

protected: _____

_____

unique: _____

_____

popular: _____

_____

1 What does the word beautiful mean?

There are many beautiful and interesting fish to be seen.

- Ⓐ Lacks beauty
- Ⓑ Has the most beauty
- Ⓒ Has more beauty
- Ⓓ Full of beauty

2 Which sentence from the passage is a fact?
- Ⓐ *It is the largest reef in the world.*
- Ⓑ *It is important that the reef is not lost.*
- Ⓒ *It is too unique and special to be lost.*
- Ⓓ *There are many beautiful and interesting fish to be seen.*

3 What would be the best thing to add to the passage to show where the Great Barrier Reef is located?
- Ⓐ A graph
- Ⓑ A timeline
- Ⓒ A map
- Ⓓ A table

4 The passage states that the reef has been called "one of the seven natural wonders of the world." Which claim does this detail best support?
- Ⓐ The reef is found off the coast of Australia.
- Ⓑ The reef is made up of many smaller reefs and islands.
- Ⓒ The reef is protected.
- Ⓓ The reef is unique and special.

My Day at the Zoo

I went to the zoo today with my big sister. We saw lions, tigers, and penguins. My sister liked the chimps the best because they could swing in the trees. I liked the tigers the most. They were so big and reminded me of my pet cat. I don't think Mom would let a tiger sleep on our couch!

The only animals I didn't like were the snakes. Some of them were huge. They looked like they might wrap themselves around me and squeeze until there was nothing left of me. They were safely behind glass, but they still scared me a bit. My big sister and I had a great day at the zoo. We took lots of pictures to show everybody else that could not come.

CORE SKILLS PRACTICE

The writer describes the tigers by saying they were "so big." This description does not help the reader imagine the tigers. Look at the picture of a tiger. Write a description of the tiger. Include details that would help someone imagine what the tiger looks like.

_____

_____

_____

_____

_____

_____

1   Read this sentence from the passage.

   I don't think Mom would let a tiger sleep on our couch!

   Which word means about the same as <u>couch</u>?

   Ⓐ   Floor
   Ⓑ   Lawn
   Ⓒ   Sofa
   Ⓓ   Rug

2   Which word would the narrator most likely use to describe her day at the zoo?

   Ⓐ   Tiring
   Ⓑ   Fun
   Ⓒ   Boring
   Ⓓ   Silly

3   Complete the diagram below by writing the missing reasons.

Character's Feelings	Reason for the Feelings
The big sister liked the chimps the most.	The chimps swung in the trees.
The narrator liked the tigers the most.	
The narrator was scared of the snakes.	

Everyone Loves Cake

Tomorrow I will bake a cake. Last time I tried to make a cake, it was a disaster. It was gooey and undercooked and it was far too sweet. I know everything went wrong because I was rushing. I didn't measure the ingredients properly and I used brown sugar instead of normal sugar. I didn't preheat the oven and I didn't time it. I put the frosting on right away and it melted and ran everywhere. This time I am going to be organized. Today I must first get everything ready.

I need eggs, milk, flour, and sugar. Mom is going to buy some mixing bowls and a tin for the cake. I am going to mix everything together. Then I will pour it into the cake tin. Mom is going to help put the cake in the oven because it can get very hot. I do not want to drop the cake or hurt myself.

She will take the cake out of the oven after exactly an hour. I will set the timer, so I'll know when it's time to take the cake out. Once the cake is cool, we are going to cover it with pink frosting. It will look delicious! I am sure Mom will also help me by eating some of it!

CORE SKILLS PRACTICE

The writer of the passage describes how she is going to make the cake. Complete the list of steps for making the cake.

1. Mix the eggs, milk, flour, and sugar together.

2. Pour the mixture into a cake tin.

3. _____

4. _____

5. _____

6. Put frosting on the cake.

1 Read this sentence from the passage.

Once the cake is cool, we are going to cover it with pink frosting.

Which word means the opposite of <u>cool</u>?

- Ⓐ Raw
- Ⓑ Cold
- Ⓒ Ready
- Ⓓ Warm

2 Which statement is most likely true about the narrator?

- Ⓐ She has made cakes many times before.
- Ⓑ She is worried about ruining the cake.
- Ⓒ She is not looking forward to eating the cake.
- Ⓓ She does not like eating sweet foods.

3 Which of the following is NOT needed to make the cake?

- Ⓐ Milk
- Ⓑ Eggs
- Ⓒ Butter
- Ⓓ Sugar

4 The main lesson of the passage is about —

- Ⓐ overcoming your fears
- Ⓑ learning from your mistakes
- Ⓒ doing good deeds for others
- Ⓓ asking people for help

5 Describe **two** examples of things that went wrong with the first cake the narrator made. Describe what the narrator is planning to do to stop each thing going wrong. Use information from the passage in your answer.

Reading Comprehension

Set 10

Literary and Informational Texts

Instructions

Read each passage. Complete the exercise under each passage.

Then complete the questions following each passage. For each multiple-choice question, fill in the circle for the correct answer. For other types of questions, follow the instructions given. Some of the questions require a written answer. Write your answer on the lines provided.

Making Goo

It is fun to make and play with goo! It is very important that you only play with the goo. The goo should never be eaten, as it is not food. Here is how you do it:

Step 1
Mix two tablespoons of craft glue and two tablespoons of water in a cup.
(It is best to use cups that you can throw away, as it can be hard to clean up!)

Step 2
In a different cup, add 12 drops of food coloring. You can use any color or mix two colors together! Green is a popular color for goo, but you can make it any color you like.

Step 3
Add a teaspoon of detergent to half a cup of water. Add this mixture to the food coloring.

Step 4
Add both mixtures together. Then stir until it takes on the texture of goo. It should feel slippery and slimy.

Your goo is now ready for you to have fun with. The fun thing about goo is how horrible and slimy it feels! You can shape it and squeeze it. You can dare people to touch it or have goo fights with your friends.

CORE SKILLS PRACTICE

What does the picture help the reader understand about the goo?

_____

_____

_____

_____

1   In Step 4, which word could best be used in place of <u>texture</u>?

      Ⓐ   Look

      Ⓑ   Feel

      Ⓒ   Smell

      Ⓓ   Taste

2   Why does the author tell readers that goo is not food?

      Ⓐ   To show what goo looks like

      Ⓑ   To warn that the goo should not be eaten

      Ⓒ   To explain how to make goo

      Ⓓ   To show that goo does not need to be cooked

3   Write the numbers 1, 2, 3, and 4 on the lines to place the steps below in order from first to last.

      ___   Adding the detergent to the water

      ___   Mixing the craft glue and the water

      ___   Adding drops of food coloring

      ___   Stirring the mixture until it is like goo

4   Which sentence from the passage gives a suggestion?

      Ⓐ   *It is very important that you only play with the goo.*

      Ⓑ   *In a different cup, add 12 drops of food coloring.*

      Ⓒ   *Green is a popular color for goo, but you can make it any color you like.*

      Ⓓ   *The fun thing about goo is how horrible and slimy it feels!*

Gorillas

Gorillas are an endangered species. This means that there are not many gorillas left in the world.

Gorillas are herbivores. Herbivores are animals that eat only plants. Gorillas eat about 65 pounds of plants a day. That's a lot of vegetables! They enjoy green leafy plants and bamboo the most.

It is important to keep their habitats safe from harm. This will help make sure they can find enough food to eat. This will help them continue to live for a long time.

CORE SKILLS PRACTICE

The passage describes what some words mean. Locate the two words below in the passage. Write a sentence explaining what each word means.

endangered: _____

_____

herbivore: _____

_____

1 As it is used in the sentence below, what does the word <u>habitat</u> mean?

It is important to keep their habitat safe from harm.

- Ⓐ The place where animals live
- Ⓑ What animals eat
- Ⓒ Actions that are done often
- Ⓓ To be free from danger

2 What does the illustration best show?
- Ⓐ Where gorillas live
- Ⓑ How many gorillas are left
- Ⓒ What gorillas eat
- Ⓓ Why gorillas are endangered

3 Which sentence from the passage is an opinion?
- Ⓐ *Gorillas are an endangered species.*
- Ⓑ *Gorillas are herbivores.*
- Ⓒ *Gorillas eat about 65 pounds of plants a day.*
- Ⓓ *It is important to keep their habitats safe from harm.*

4 What extra information would be most useful in the passage to help readers understand how to protect gorilla habitats?
- Ⓐ Details about how much water gorillas need
- Ⓑ Details about how gorillas take care of their young
- Ⓒ Details about whether gorillas can be dangerous
- Ⓓ Details about where gorillas are found

A Happy Day

I went to my friend Jema's house today. I often visit her on the weekend. Sometimes we swim in the pool or hang out in her treehouse. It was raining today, so we couldn't do those things.

"Let's watch a movie," Jema suggested. "You're my guest Katy, so you can pick it."

I picked a movie called *Dance of Joy*. The movie was about a girl called Susan who liked to dance. She was a ballerina. Susan had a cat named Albert. Albert chewed her ballet shoes, so she could not dance anymore. It made me sad, but then Albert found Susan some new ballet shoes to wear. Albert surprised Susan by bringing her the new shoes in his mouth. It was a wonderful happy ending.

I told Jema I loved the movie. She laughed and said she had found it completely boring. She had only kept watching it because I looked like I was enjoying it so much. I felt a little bad about it, but it's nice to have a good friend like Jema.

CORE SKILLS PRACTICE

The third paragraph is a summary of the movie. It describes the main events of the movie. Think of a movie you have watched, or a book you have read. Write a summary of the book or movie.

_____

_____

_____

_____

_____

_____

1. Read this sentence from the passage.

   It was a wonderful happy ending.

   Which word means the opposite of <u>wonderful</u>?
   - Ⓐ   Terrible
   - Ⓑ   Nice
   - Ⓒ   Surprising
   - Ⓓ   Perfect

2. Who is telling the story?
   - Ⓐ   Jema
   - Ⓑ   Susan
   - Ⓒ   Albert
   - Ⓓ   Katy

3. What does Albert do to Susan's ballet shoes?
   - Ⓐ   Hides them
   - Ⓑ   Dirties them
   - Ⓒ   Chews them
   - Ⓓ   Finds them

4. Which sentence from the passage best shows Jema's kindness?
   - Ⓐ   *I went to my friend Jema's house today.*
   - Ⓑ   *Sometimes we swim in the pool or hang out in her treehouse.*
   - Ⓒ   *She laughed and said she had found it completely boring.*
   - Ⓓ   *She had only kept watching it because I looked like I was enjoying it so much.*

It's Hailing, It's Pouring

Balls of ice that fall from the sky during a storm are known as hail. Hail is caused when the clouds in the sky are high enough to cause rain water to freeze. Many people say that you know when it is about to hail because the clouds turn slightly green. Hail storms do not last long, but a lot of hail can fall in a short time.

The largest hailstone in the United States weighed 1.93 pounds. It was about the size of a bowling ball. It fell in South Dakota on July 23, 2010. Most hail is not this large, but hail about the size of golf balls is not uncommon. Hail can also fall from the sky at very high speeds.

Hail can cause a lot of damage to houses, cars, and of course, people. It's important to find a safe place to take cover during a hail storm. If you're indoors, you should also stay away from windows.

CORE SKILLS PRACTICE

Look at the photograph in the passage. Explain what it helps readers understand about hail. How does it help show that hail can cause a lot of damage?

_____

_____

_____

_____

_____

_____

1   According to the passage, which of the following would show that it is about to hail?

    Ⓐ   Light rain
    Ⓑ   Green clouds
    Ⓒ   Lightning
    Ⓓ   Thunder

2   Which clouds are most likely to produce hail?

    Ⓐ   Small ones
    Ⓑ   Large ones
    Ⓒ   Low ones
    Ⓓ   High ones

3   Read this sentence from the passage.

    It was about the size of a bowling ball.

    Why did the author include this sentence?

    Ⓐ   To suggest that the hail rolled easily
    Ⓑ   To help readers imagine how large the hail was
    Ⓒ   To show that the hail was very heavy
    Ⓓ   To warn readers of the dangers of hail

4   The author states that hail can "fall from the sky at very high speeds." What is the main reason this detail is important?

    Ⓐ   It explains why hail storms do not last long.
    Ⓑ   It explains why hail can cause a lot of damage.
    Ⓒ   It explains why hail the size of golf balls is not uncommon.
    Ⓓ   It explains why hail only forms when rain water freezes.

5 Why is hail dangerous? In your answer, explain how it could harm people. Use information from the passage to support your answer.

Reading Comprehension

Set 11

Paired Literary Texts

Instructions

This set contains a pair of passages. Read each passage on its own first. Complete the exercise under each passage. Then complete the questions following each passage.

For each multiple-choice question, fill in the circle for the correct answer. For other types of questions, follow the instructions given. Some of the questions require a written answer. Write your answer on the lines provided.

After reading both passages, you will answer one or more additional questions. You will use information from both passages to answer these questions. Write your answers on the lines provided.

Animals of the Night

The sun has set. All of the birds are going to sleep. There is no longer the sound of chirping or singing. Leaves float around and blow down the city streets. The trees begin to sway in the wind.

Soon, the animals of the night will come out to play. The animals can be very loud. They may call out to each other. They will sometimes find a roof to run across, waking up sleeping humans. The humans stir and wonder what the sound is above them. Then they drift off to sleep as the animals continue their play.

CORE SKILLS PRACTICE

In this story, the author gives many details that describe the sounds of the night. Think of a different scene you could describe using sound. It might be a busy street, a quiet classroom, or a noisy parade. Describe that scene. Use details that will help the reader imagine the sounds.

_____

_____

_____

_____

_____

_____

1. Which word means about the same as <u>sway</u>?

   The trees begin to sway in the wind.

   Ⓐ　Creak

   Ⓑ　Bend

   Ⓒ　Break

   Ⓓ　Rest

2. What is the mood of the first paragraph?

   Ⓐ　Peaceful

   Ⓑ　Scary

   Ⓒ　Sad

   Ⓓ　Excited

3. According to the passage, what can wake up humans?

   Ⓐ　Animals running on a roof

   Ⓑ　Trees creaking in the wind

   Ⓒ　Animals calling out to each other

   Ⓓ　Birds chirping and singing

4. Which phrase from the last sentences creates a feeling of calm?

   Ⓐ　*wonder what the sound*

   Ⓑ　*above them*

   Ⓒ　*drift off*

   Ⓓ　*continue their play*

Stormy Night

There were gray clouds moving slowly over the farm. The sky was getting dark and the wind was starting to howl. The trees were bending and creaking. The windows of the house were rattling in the wind. Some of the animals were scared, but not the cow. The cow was safe and warm in the barn.

The chickens and some sheep were also in the barn. Farmer Paul just finished getting the other animals to a safe place when it began to rain. The storm had begun. Now that the animals were safe, Farmer John raced through the rain back to his house. He was just inside the front door when the first streak of lightning split the sky in two. He took off his coat, got out the candles, and settled in for a long night.

CORE SKILLS PRACTICE

In the passage, the author wants the reader to be able to imagine the storm. The author gives details describing what the storm looked and sounded like. Complete the table below by listing the details the author gives.

Sight of the clouds	gray and moving slowly
Sight of the sky	
Sound of the wind	
Sound of the bending trees	
Sound of the windows	

5   Which words from the passage create a feeling of comfort?
    Ⓐ   *getting dark*
    Ⓑ   *starting to howl*
    Ⓒ   *safe and warm*
    Ⓓ   *in the barn*

6   How would the animals outside most likely feel during the storm?
    Ⓐ   Calm
    Ⓑ   Afraid
    Ⓒ   Excited
    Ⓓ   Safe

7   Which of the following is NOT described in the passage?
    Ⓐ   Howling wind
    Ⓑ   Dark sky
    Ⓒ   Gray clouds
    Ⓓ   Loud thunder

8   The author describes how the "first streak of lightning split the sky in two." What is the main purpose of this image?
    Ⓐ   To warn of the damage that lightning can do
    Ⓑ   To suggest that Farmer John is separated from his animals
    Ⓒ   To emphasize how powerful the lightning is
    Ⓓ   To show that Farmer John will not need the candles

9 How does Farmer Paul show kindness in the passage? Use information from the passage to support your answer.

Directions: Use both passages to answer the following questions.

10   Compare the settings of the two passages. Describe **one** way they are similar and **one** way they are different.

_____

_____

_____

_____

_____

_____

_____

11   In which passage are the animals described as if they have human feelings? Explain your answer.

_____

_____

_____

_____

_____

_____

12 Think about the relationship between animals and humans described in the passages. In which passage are humans most important to the animals? Use information from both passages to explain your answer.

Reading Comprehension

Set 12

Paired Informational Texts

Instructions

This set contains a pair of passages. Read each passage on its own first. Complete the exercise under each passage. Then complete the questions following each passage.

For each multiple-choice question, fill in the circle for the correct answer. For other types of questions, follow the instructions given. Some of the questions require a written answer. Write your answer on the lines provided.

After reading both passages, you will answer one or more additional questions. You will use information from both passages to answer these questions. Write your answers on the lines provided.

Recycling is Important

Recycling is important. Recycling helps keep our planet healthy. Many different things can be recycled. These include plastic bottles, glass bottles, tin cans, and paper.

They are broken down and then used to make new things. This is good because the new things take much less energy to make. It also decreases the amount of waste. It's better for old items to be used to make new things than to be stored in huge rubbish dumps!

If you want to help, make sure your household recycles as much as possible. Know all the types of things that can be recycled and be sure to sort the recycled items if you need to. You might have one bin for paper, one for plastic, and one for glass bottles. You could even recycle old food scraps by using them to make compost. You'll have less waste and a healthy garden. That's the thing about recycling – it often helps you and the environment at the same time.

CORE SKILLS PRACTICE

The author states that recycling is important. The author then gives reasons that recycling is important. These reasons support the idea that recycling is important. Complete the chart below by listing **two** more supporting details.

Idea	Supporting Details
Recycling is important.	It keeps the planet healthy.

1 Complete the web below using information from the passage.

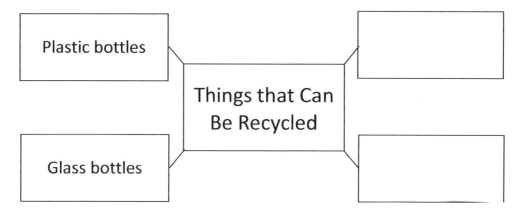

2 What is the main purpose of the passage?
- Ⓐ To tell a story about recycling
- Ⓑ To explain how items are recycled
- Ⓒ To teach people how to recycle paper
- Ⓓ To persuade people to recycle

3 Which sentence from the passage best summarizes the main message?
- Ⓐ *Recycling helps keep our planet healthy.*
- Ⓑ *They are broken down and then used to make new things.*
- Ⓒ *This is good because the new things take much less energy to make.*
- Ⓓ *It also decreases the amount of waste.*

4 How is the example of recycling food scraps different from recycling paper, plastic, and glass bottles?
- Ⓐ The food scraps do not need to be sorted.
- Ⓑ You recycle the food scraps yourself.
- Ⓒ The recycling helps the environment.
- Ⓓ It is a way of reducing waste.

Saving Water

Water is very important for people. The human body is made up of 70 percent water. People need to drink water every day to stay healthy. Water is also used to help grow the plants that people eat. This means it is very important that we keep our water clean and use it only when we need to.

Some people think there is nothing they can do, but that's not true. Every single person should do what they can. It might not seem like a lot, but every positive action adds up. If everyone did something, our water would be much cleaner and there would be enough for everybody.

You can help keep water clean by not littering in public and always using a trash bin. You can also make sure you never pour oil down the sink. It is also important not to waste water. Here are four tips for water use:

- Turn off the tap when you brush your teeth
- Take shorter showers
- Only do full washing loads
- Water the garden in the early evening

CORE SKILLS PRACTICE

The author thinks that it is important to save water. Do you agree that it is important to save water? Explain why you do or do not agree.

_____

_____

_____

_____

_____

5 According to the passage, what is one way to keep water clean?

- Ⓐ Using water to water plants
- Ⓑ Not pouring oil down the sink
- Ⓒ Doing full washing loads
- Ⓓ Drinking water every day

6 What is the main purpose of the bullet points?

- Ⓐ To explain why water is important
- Ⓑ To list ways to save water
- Ⓒ To show common uses of water
- Ⓓ To describe how to keep water clean

7 Which sentence best shows that water is important to people?

- Ⓐ *People need to drink water every day to stay healthy.*
- Ⓑ *It is also important that we use water only when we need to.*
- Ⓒ *You can help keep water clean by not littering.*
- Ⓓ *You can also make sure you never pour oil down the sink.*

8 Which of these is a message of the passage?

- Ⓐ Little things can make a big difference.
- Ⓑ The best things in life are free.
- Ⓒ You should share your knowledge with others.
- Ⓓ Everyone makes mistakes sometimes.

Directions: Use both passages to answer the following question.

9   Describe how people can make simple changes to help the environment. Use information from both passages in your answer.

_____

_____

_____

_____

_____

_____

_____

_____

_____

_____

_____

_____

_____

_____

ANSWER KEY

Common Core State Standards

The state of New Jersey has adopted the Common Core State Standards. These standards describe what students are expected to know. Student learning throughout the year is based on these standards, and all the questions on the state tests assess these standards.

All the exercises and questions in this book cover the Common Core State Standards. This book will develop all the Common Core reading skills, as well as complementary writing and language skills.

Core Skills Practice

Each passage includes an exercise focused on one key skill described in the Common Core standards. The answer key identifies the core skill covered by each exercise, and describes what to look for in the student's response.

Common Core Reading Standards

The Common Core reading standards are divided into the following two areas:

- Reading Standards for Literature
- Reading Standards for Informational Text

Within each of these areas, there are nine standards that describe specific skills the student should have. The answer key on the following pages lists the standard assessed by each question. The skill listed can be used to identify a student's areas of strength and weakness, so revision and instruction can be targeted accordingly.

Scoring Constructed-Response Questions

This workbook includes constructed-response questions, where students provide a written answer to a question. Short questions are scored out of 2 and longer questions are scored out of 4. The answer key gives guidance on how to score these questions. Use the criteria listed as a guide to scoring these questions, and as a guide for giving the student advice on how to improve an answer.

Set 1: Literary Texts

Robot Boy

Core Skills Practice
Core skill: Explain how information is conveyed through key details
Answer: The student should identify two ways you can tell that the narrator enjoys pretending to be a robot. The student may describe how he says it is fun, how he wears his robot suit a lot, or how he does many things in his robot suit.

Question	Answer	Common Core Reading Standard
1	A	Recount stories; determine the central message, lesson, or moral and explain how it is conveyed through key details in the text.
2	2, 1, 3, 4	Describe characters in a story (e.g., their traits, motivations, or feelings) and explain how their actions contribute to the sequence of events.
3	B	Ask and answer questions to demonstrate understanding of a text, referring explicitly to the text as the basis for the answers.
4	Step 2	Refer to parts of stories, dramas, and poems when writing or speaking about a text, using terms such as chapter, scene, and stanza; describe how each successive part builds on earlier sections.

A Special Day

Core Skills Practice
Core skill: Describe the feelings of characters in a story
Answer: The student should refer to how Brin cannot decide which four books to choose or to how she is overwhelmed by the choices. The student should relate this to how being reminded she can swap them for another four would calm her.

Question	Answer	Common Core Reading Standard
1	C	Ask and answer questions to demonstrate understanding of a text, referring explicitly to the text as the basis for the answers.
2	A	Recount stories; determine the central message, lesson, or moral and explain how it is conveyed through key details in the text.
3	A	Distinguish their own point of view from that of the narrator or those of the characters.
4	B	Explain how specific aspects of a text's illustrations contribute to what is conveyed by the words in a story.

The Car

Core Skills Practice

Core skill: Determine the central message, lesson, or moral of a text

Answer: The student should give a title that relates to the topic or message of the passage, such as "Taking Care of the Car." The student should explain why the title suits the passage.

Question	Answer	Common Core Reading Standard
1	B	Describe characters in a story (e.g., their traits, motivations, or feelings) and explain how their actions contribute to the sequence of events.
2	A	Refer to parts of stories, dramas, and poems when writing or speaking about a text, using terms such as chapter, scene, and stanza; describe how each successive part builds on earlier sections.
3	C	Determine the meaning of words and phrases as they are used in a text, distinguishing literal from nonliteral language.
4	D	Determine the meaning of words and phrases as they are used in a text, distinguishing literal from nonliteral language.

Mother Knows Best

Core Skills Practice

Core skill: Describe how a character's actions contribute to the sequence of events

Answer: The student should explain that the speaker ends up with mice in her bedroom because she did not listen to her mother. The student should explain that the mice would not have come if the speaker had of listened and not eaten food in her room.

Question	Answer	Common Core Reading Standard
1	A	Ask and answer questions to demonstrate understanding of a text, referring explicitly to the text as the basis for the answers.
2	B	Determine the meaning of words and phrases as they are used in a text, distinguishing literal from nonliteral language.
3	C	Refer to parts of stories, dramas, and poems when writing or speaking about a text, using terms such as chapter, scene, and stanza; describe how each successive part builds on earlier sections.
4	A	Recount stories; determine the central message, lesson, or moral and explain how it is conveyed through key details in the text.
5	See Below	Recount stories; determine the central message, lesson, or moral and explain how it is conveyed through key details in the text.

Give a score of 0, 1, 2, 3, or 4 based on how well the answer meets the criteria listed.
- It should identify the main message of the poem as being about listening to others, taking advice, or learning from your mistakes.
- It should use relevant details from the passage.
- It should be well-organized, clear, and easy to understand.

Set 2: Informational Texts

Mozart

Core Skills Practice
Core skill: Summarize a text
Answer: The student should write a short summary that includes the details below.
He worked as a court musician in Austria.
He looked for work and wrote music in Paris.
He wrote his best-known work in Vienna.

Question	Answer	Common Core Reading Standard
1	B	Determine the meaning of general academic and domain-specific words and phrases in a text.
2	B	Distinguish their own point of view from that of the author of a text.
3	A	Determine the main idea of a text; recount the key details and explain how they support the main idea.
4	C	Ask and answer questions to demonstrate understanding of a text, referring explicitly to the text as the basis for the answers.

Presidents

Core Skills Practice
Core skill: Form and express an opinion based on a text
Answer: The student should give plausible reasons about how being vice president first would benefit a president. The answer could refer to gaining experience, learning from the president, or taking on a similar role before taking on the full role.

Question	Answer	Common Core Reading Standard
1	B	Describe the logical connection between particular sentences and paragraphs in a text.
2	John Adams	Use text features and search tools (e.g., key words, sidebars, hyperlinks) to locate information relevant to a given topic efficiently.
3	A	Describe the relationship between a series of historical events, scientific ideas or concepts, or steps in technical procedures in a text, using language that pertains to time, sequence, and cause/effect.
4	A	Distinguish their own point of view from that of the author of a text.

Neil Armstrong

Core Skills Practice

Core skill: Understand literal and nonliteral meanings of words and phrases in context

Answer: The student should give a reasonable explanation of the meaning of the statement. The answer should refer to how it was one small step but represented great progress.

Question	Answer	Common Core Reading Standard
1	D	Distinguish their own point of view from that of the author of a text.
2	D	Distinguish their own point of view from that of the author of a text.
3	B	Determine the main idea of a text; recount the key details and explain how they support the main idea.
4	B	Describe the logical connection between particular sentences and paragraphs in a text.

Crying Over Onions

Core Skills Practice

Core skill: Describe the connection between particular sentences in a text

Answer: The student may describe how the author asks questions to get the reader thinking about the topic, or how the questions make the reader curious about onions.

Question	Answer	Common Core Reading Standard
1	B	Determine the meaning of general academic and domain-specific words and phrases in a text.
2	B	Describe the relationship between a series of historical events, scientific ideas or concepts, or steps in technical procedures in a text, using language that pertains to time, sequence, and cause/effect.
3	See Below	Ask and answer questions to demonstrate understanding of a text, referring explicitly to the text as the basis for the answers.
4	See Below	Determine the main idea of a text; recount the key details and explain how they support the main idea.

Q3.
The student should list the following: freeze the onions, wear goggles, cut the onions under a window.

Q4.
Give a score of 0, 1, 2, 3, or 4 based on how well the answer meets the criteria listed.
- It should explain why onions make people cry.
- It should describe whether it is a good thing or a bad thing that onions make people cry, and include a fully-supported explanation of why.
- It should use relevant details from the passage.
- It should be well-organized, clear, and easy to understand.

Set 3: Literary and Informational Texts

Henry the Parrot

Core Skills Practice
Core skill: Write narratives / Understand point of view
Answer: The student should write a narrative about the parrot spilling the water. The narrative should be written in third-person point of view from the mother's point of view.

Question	Answer	Common Core Reading Standard
1	B	Ask and answer questions to demonstrate understanding of a text, referring explicitly to the text as the basis for the answers.
2	D	Ask and answer questions to demonstrate understanding of a text, referring explicitly to the text as the basis for the answers.
3	D	Determine the meaning of words and phrases as they are used in a text, distinguishing literal from nonliteral language.
4	B	Recount stories; determine the central message, lesson, or moral and explain how it is conveyed through key details in the text.

An Unusual Gift

Core Skills Practice
Core skill: Answer questions by referring explicitly to a text
Answer: The student should list any four of the facts below.
- He was born in 1847.
- He invented the telephone.
- He did not have a middle name when he was born.
- He had two brothers.
- He got a middle name when he was 11.
- He was given the middle name "Graham."
- He was named after a family friend.

Question	Answer	Common Core Reading Standard
1	B	Determine the main idea of a text; recount the key details and explain how they support the main idea.
2	A	Determine the meaning of general academic and domain-specific words and phrases in a text.
3	D	Distinguish their own point of view from that of the author of a text.
4	B	Describe the logical connection between particular sentences and paragraphs in a text.

Soil

Core Skills Practice

Core skill: Use information gained from illustrations

Answer: The student may explain that the photograph shows soil in a desert that is very dry, and that it shows that few plants live in this soil.

Question	Answer	Common Core Reading Standard
1	B	Determine the meaning of general academic and domain-specific words and phrases in a text.
2	D	Ask and answer questions to demonstrate understanding of a text, referring explicitly to the text as the basis for the answers.
3	D	Describe the logical connection between particular sentences and paragraphs in a text.
4	See Below	Describe the relationship between a series of historical events, scientific ideas or concepts, or steps in technical procedures in a text, using language that pertains to time, sequence, and cause/effect.

The student should list the following: They make soil softer. They help water drain.

Stewart the Dragon

Core Skills Practice

Core skill: Determine the central message, lesson, or moral of a text

Answer: The student should identify the theme as being about accepting others, not judging others, the problem of feeling lonely, or how important it is to spend time with people.

Question	Answer	Common Core Reading Standard
1	C	Ask and answer questions to demonstrate understanding of a text, referring explicitly to the text as the basis for the answers.
2	B	Recount stories; determine the central message, lesson, or moral and explain how it is conveyed through key details in the text.
3	A	Describe characters in a story (e.g., their traits, motivations, or feelings) and explain how their actions contribute to the sequence of events.
4	D	Refer to parts of stories, dramas, and poems when writing or speaking about a text, using terms such as chapter, scene, and stanza; describe how each successive part builds on earlier sections.
5	See Below	Recount stories; determine the central message, lesson, or moral and explain how it is conveyed through key details in the text.

Give a score of 0, 1, 2, 3, or 4 based on how well the answer meets the criteria listed.
- It should describe how the people of the town are scared of Stewart at the start.
- It should explain how the people end up liking or accepting Stewart.
- It should use relevant details from the passage.
- It should be well-organized, clear, and easy to understand.

Reading Comprehension, Common Core Workbook, Grade 3

Set 4: Literary and Informational Texts

A Letter to Grandma

Core Skills Practice
Core skill: Answer questions by referring explicitly to a text
Answer: The student should answer the questions based on the information in the passage.
- The school fair was held on the football fields.
- Anna won a key ring.
- Anna got her face painted as a cat.
- Anna bought choc chip cookies.

Question	Answer	Common Core Reading Standard
1	C	Determine the meaning of words and phrases as they are used in a text, distinguishing literal from nonliteral language.
2	A	Distinguish their own point of view from that of the narrator or those of the characters.
3	D	Ask and answer questions to demonstrate understanding of a text, referring explicitly to the text as the basis for the answers.
4	See Below	Recount stories; determine the central message, lesson, or moral and explain how it is conveyed through key details in the text.

The student should list any of the following: went on rides, played darts, won a key ring, got her face painted, bought cookies.

Sound

Core Skills Practice
Core skill: Describe the connection between paragraphs in a text
Answer: The student should identify the main topic of the second paragraph as being about how sounds travel in water, and the main topic of the third paragraph as being about how people and animals use sound.

Question	Answer	Common Core Reading Standard
1	C	Use information gained from illustrations and the words in a text to demonstrate understanding of the text.
2	C	Ask and answer questions to demonstrate understanding of a text, referring explicitly to the text as the basis for the answers.
3	B	Describe the logical connection between particular sentences and paragraphs in a text.
4	C	Describe the relationship between a series of historical events, scientific ideas or concepts, or steps in technical procedures in a text, using language that pertains to time, sequence, and cause/effect.

Reading Comprehension, Common Core Workbook, Grade 3

A Fresh Coat of Paint

Core Skills Practice

Core skill: Form and express an opinion based on a text

Answer: The student should explain whether or not the father's solution was a good one, and provide reasons to support the opinion.

Question	Answer	Common Core Reading Standard
1	C	Recount stories; determine the central message, lesson, or moral and explain how it is conveyed through key details in the text.
2	C	Ask and answer questions to demonstrate understanding of a text, referring explicitly to the text as the basis for the answers.
3	A	Describe characters in a story (e.g., their traits, motivations, or feelings) and explain how their actions contribute to the sequence of events.
4	B	Refer to parts of stories, dramas, and poems when writing or speaking about a text, using terms such as chapter, scene, and stanza; describe how each successive part builds on earlier sections.

Deviled Eggs

Core Skills Practice

Core skill: Write an informative text

Answer: The student should describe the steps in making a snack or meal in order.

Question	Answer	Common Core Reading Standard
1	A	Use information gained from illustrations and the words in a text to demonstrate understanding of the text.
2	A	Determine the main idea of a text; recount the key details and explain how they support the main idea.
3	C	Use text features and search tools (e.g., key words, sidebars, hyperlinks) to locate information relevant to a given topic efficiently.
4	D	Describe the relationship between a series of historical events, scientific ideas or concepts, or steps in technical procedures in a text, using language that pertains to time, sequence, and cause/effect.
5	See Below	Distinguish their own point of view from that of the author of a text.

Give a score of 0, 1, 2, 3, or 4 based on how well the answer meets the criteria listed.
- It should state an opinion of whether or not deviled eggs would be easy to make.
- It should provide a fully-supported explanation of why deviled eggs would or would not be easy to make.
- It should use relevant details from the passage.
- It should be well-organized, clear, and easy to understand.

Set 5: Paired Literary Texts

Bread and Milk/Missing

Core Skills Practice
Core skill: Summarize a text
Answer: The summary should include that Niral did not have enough money for the bread and milk, and that the shopkeeper said she could have the items for five dollars.

Core Skills Practice
Core skill: Explain how information is conveyed through key details
Answer: The student should explain how James's actions show how keen he is. The answer may refer to how he looks frazzled, to his actions as he looks for it, or how he will not give up.

Question	Answer	Common Core Reading Standard
1	A	Describe characters in a story (e.g., their traits, motivations, or feelings) and explain how their actions contribute to the sequence of events.
2	A	Recount stories; determine the central message, lesson, or moral and explain how it is conveyed through key details in the text.
3	C	Describe characters in a story (e.g., their traits, motivations, or feelings) and explain how their actions contribute to the sequence of events.
4	D	Refer to parts of stories, dramas, and poems when writing or speaking about a text, using terms such as chapter, scene, and stanza; describe how each successive part builds on earlier sections.
5	A	Determine the meaning of words and phrases as they are used in a text, distinguishing literal from nonliteral language.
6	C	Ask and answer questions to demonstrate understanding of a text, referring explicitly to the text as the basis for the answers.
7	A	Recount stories; determine the central message, lesson, or moral and explain how it is conveyed through key details in the text.
8	C	Describe characters in a story (e.g., their traits, motivations, or feelings) and explain how their actions contribute to the sequence of events.
9	See Below	Compare and contrast the themes, settings, and plots of stories written by the same author about the same or similar characters.
10	See Below	Compare and contrast the themes, settings, and plots of stories written by the same author about the same or similar characters.

Q9.
Give a score of 0, 1, or 2 based on how well the answer meets the criteria listed.
- It should refer to how the shopkeeper and Sarah are both kind or both help someone.

Q10.
Give a score of 0, 1, or 2 based on how well the answer meets the criteria listed.
- It should describe how Niral does not have enough money and how James has lost something.
- It should give an opinion on which problem is the most serious and explain why.

Set 6: Paired Informational Texts

Jupiter/Poor Pluto

Core Skills Practice
Core skill: Contrast two items / Locate relevant information
Answer: The student should complete the table with the following details about Jupiter.
Fifth planet from the Sun / 16 moons / Surface made of gases

Core Skills Practice
Core skill: Summarize key information in a text
Answer: Differences include that Pluto is smaller, colder, farther from the Sun, or is a dwarf planet.

Question	Answer	Common Core Reading Standard
1	C	Determine the meaning of general academic and domain-specific words and phrases in a text.
2	B	Determine the main idea of a text; recount the key details and explain how they support the main idea.
3	D	Describe the relationship between a series of historical events, scientific ideas or concepts, or steps in technical procedures in a text, using language that pertains to time, sequence, and cause/effect.
4	D	Use information gained from illustrations and the words in a text to demonstrate understanding of the text.
5	A	Distinguish their own point of view from that of the author of a text.
6	C	Describe the relationship between a series of historical events, scientific ideas or concepts, or steps in technical procedures in a text, using language that pertains to time, sequence, and cause/effect.
7	D	Determine the main idea of a text; recount the key details and explain how they support the main idea.
8	C	Use information gained from illustrations and the words in a text to demonstrate understanding of the text.
9	See Below	Compare and contrast the most important points and key details presented in two texts on the same topic.
10	See Below	Compare and contrast the most important points and key details presented in two texts on the same topic.

Q9.
Give a score of 0, 1, or 2 based on how well the answer meets the criteria listed.
- It should explain why it is difficult to study Pluto and Jupiter. It should refer to how Pluto and Jupiter are far away, and may refer to how spacecraft cannot land on Jupiter.

Q10.
Give a score of 0, 1, or 2 based on how well the answer meets the criteria listed.
- It should explain that patience is needed because it takes many years to reach the planets.
- It may refer to how it takes about 5 years for a spacecraft to reach Jupiter and about 10 years for a spacecraft to reach Pluto.

Set 7: Literary Texts

Animal Noises

Core Skills Practice
Core skill: Determine the purpose of a text
Answer: The student should identify that the poem is meant to be funny and give evidence to support the opinion. The student may refer to the funny noises described, the art, or the playful tone.

Question	Answer	Common Core Reading Standard
1	C	Explain how specific aspects of a text's illustrations contribute to what is conveyed by the words in a story.
2	B	Refer to parts of stories, dramas, and poems when writing or speaking about a text, using terms such as chapter, scene, and stanza; describe how each successive part builds on earlier sections.
3	A	Determine the meaning of words and phrases as they are used in a text, distinguishing literal from nonliteral language.
4	B	Recount stories; determine the central message, lesson, or moral and explain how it is conveyed through key details in the text.

My Duck Family

Core Skills Practice
Core skill: Write narratives / Understand point of view
Answer: The student should write a narrative about an animal. The narrative should be written in first-person point of view with the animal as the narrator.

Question	Answer	Common Core Reading Standard
1	A	Determine the meaning of words and phrases as they are used in a text, distinguishing literal from nonliteral language.
2	A	Distinguish their own point of view from that of the narrator or those of the characters.
3	C	Ask and answer questions to demonstrate understanding of a text, referring explicitly to the text as the basis for the answers.
4	B	Describe characters in a story (e.g., their traits, motivations, or feelings) and explain how their actions contribute to the sequence of events.

Reading Comprehension, Common Core Workbook, Grade 3

Sports Day

Core Skills Practice
Core skill: Form and express an opinion based on a text
Answer: The student should explain whether or not the teacher was fair, and provide reasons to support the opinion.

Question	Answer	Common Core Reading Standard
1	B	Determine the meaning of words and phrases as they are used in a text, distinguishing literal from nonliteral language.
2	B	Ask and answer questions to demonstrate understanding of a text, referring explicitly to the text as the basis for the answers.
3	A	Recount stories; determine the central message, lesson, or moral and explain how it is conveyed through key details in the text.
4	A	Refer to parts of stories, dramas, and poems when writing or speaking about a text, using terms such as chapter, scene, and stanza; describe how each successive part builds on earlier sections.

To the Moon

Core Skills Practice
Core skill: Form and express a personal opinion
Answer: The student should express an opinion about why being an astronaut is a popular career choice.

Question	Answer	Common Core Reading Standard
1	B	Determine the meaning of words and phrases as they are used in a text, distinguishing literal from nonliteral language.
2	B	Describe characters in a story (e.g., their traits, motivations, or feelings) and explain how their actions contribute to the sequence of events.
3	C	Refer to parts of stories, dramas, and poems when writing or speaking about a text, using terms such as chapter, scene, and stanza; describe how each successive part builds on earlier sections.
4	C	Refer to parts of stories, dramas, and poems when writing or speaking about a text, using terms such as chapter, scene, and stanza; describe how each successive part builds on earlier sections.
5	See Below	Ask and answer questions to demonstrate understanding of a text, referring explicitly to the text as the basis for the answers.

Give a score of 0, 1, 2, 3, or 4 based on how well the answer meets the criteria listed.
- It should state an opinion of whether or not Jin is serious about becoming an astronaut.
- It should include a fully-supported explanation of why the student believes this.
- It should use relevant details from the passage.
- It should be well-organized, clear, and easy to understand.

Reading Comprehension, Common Core Workbook, Grade 3

Set 8: Informational Texts

Stingrays

Core Skills Practice
Core skill: Use information gained from illustrations
Answer: The student may explain that the photograph shows that stingrays live in the sea, have long flat bodies, have large fins, glide through the water, or have a stinger on their tail.

Question	Answer	Common Core Reading Standard
1	A	Use information gained from illustrations and the words in a text to demonstrate understanding of the text.
2	A	Ask and answer questions to demonstrate understanding of a text, referring explicitly to the text as the basis for the answers.
3	C	Determine the main idea of a text; recount the key details and explain how they support the main idea.
4	D	Describe the relationship between a series of historical events, scientific ideas or concepts, or steps in technical procedures in a text, using language that pertains to time, sequence, and cause/effect.

Basketball

Core Skills Practice
Core skill: Make inferences based on a text / Relate prior knowledge to a text
Answer: The student should make a valid inference about why most professional basketball players are over 6 feet tall. The inference may be based on the information in the passage or the student's prior knowledge.

Question	Answer	Common Core Reading Standard
1	C	Determine the meaning of general academic and domain-specific words and phrases in a text.
2	A	Determine the main idea of a text; recount the key details and explain how they support the main idea.
3	5	Ask and answer questions to demonstrate understanding of a text, referring explicitly to the text as the basis for the answers.
4	fifth	Distinguish their own point of view from that of the author of a text.

Turtles

Core Skills Practice

Core skill: Contrast two items / Locate relevant information

Answer: The student should list three differences between tortoises and turtles. Differences include that tortoises live mostly on land, look different, and are larger.

Question	Answer	Common Core Reading Standard
1	B	Describe the logical connection between particular sentences and paragraphs in a text.
2	B	Determine the main idea of a text; recount the key details and explain how they support the main idea.
3	C	Ask and answer questions to demonstrate understanding of a text, referring explicitly to the text as the basis for the answers.
4	B	Determine the meaning of general academic and domain-specific words and phrases in a text.

Bones

Core Skills Practice

Core skill: Determine the purpose or message of a text

Answer: The student should explain that the author wants to persuade readers to have healthy bones. The student may describe how the author wants people to eat enough foods that contain calcium.

Question	Answer	Common Core Reading Standard
1	D	Determine the meaning of general academic and domain-specific words and phrases in a text.
2	See Below	Ask and answer questions to demonstrate understanding of a text, referring explicitly to the text as the basis for the answers.
3	B	Describe the relationship between a series of historical events, scientific ideas or concepts, or steps in technical procedures in a text, using language that pertains to time, sequence, and cause/effect.
4	See Below	Determine the main idea of a text; recount the key details and explain how they support the main idea.

Q2.
The web should be completed with any of the following: cheese, yogurt, broccoli, shellfish, sardines.

Q4.
Give a score of 0, 1, 2, 3, or 4 based on how well the answer meets the criteria listed.
- It should explain how to have healthy bones.
- It should describe what you should have in your diet to have healthy bones.
- It should use relevant details from the passage.
- It should be well-organized, clear, and easy to understand.

Set 9: Literary and Informational Texts

Painted Eggs

Core Skills Practice
Core skill: Describe the connection between sentences and paragraphs in a text
Answer: The student should explain that organizing the information in steps does suit the passage. The student should relate the ordering to the purpose of the passage.

Question	Answer	Common Core Reading Standard
1	B	Describe the relationship between a series of historical events, scientific ideas or concepts, or steps in technical procedures in a text, using language that pertains to time, sequence, and cause/effect.
2	A	Use text features and search tools (e.g., key words, sidebars, hyperlinks) to locate information relevant to a given topic efficiently.
3	A	Use information gained from illustrations and the words in a text to demonstrate understanding of the text.
4	B	Determine the meaning of general academic and domain-specific words and phrases in a text.

The Great Barrier Reef

Core Skills Practice
Core skill: Determine the meaning of words and phrases in a text
Answer: The student should write a valid definition of each word. Examples are given below.
protected: not allowed to be harmed
unique: special or different
popular: liked by many people

Question	Answer	Common Core Reading Standard
1	D	Determine the meaning of general academic and domain-specific words and phrases in a text.
2	A	Distinguish their own point of view from that of the author of a text.
3	C	Use information gained from illustrations and the words in a text to demonstrate understanding of the text.
4	D	Determine the main idea of a text; recount the key details and explain how they support the main idea.

My Day at the Zoo

Core Skills Practice

Core skill: Write narratives using descriptive details

Answer: The student should write a clear description of the tiger that includes details about what the tiger looks like.

Question	Answer	Common Core Reading Standard
1	C	Determine the meaning of words and phrases as they are used in a text, distinguishing literal from nonliteral language.
2	B	Describe characters in a story (e.g., their traits, motivations, or feelings) and explain how their actions contribute to the sequence of events.
3	See Below	Ask and answer questions to demonstrate understanding of a text, referring explicitly to the text as the basis for the answers.

The chart should be completed with the following: The tigers were like her cat. The snakes looked like they might squeeze her.

Everyone Loves Cake

Core Skills Practice

Core skill: Summarize a text

Answer: The student should complete the missing steps as shown below.
3. Put the cake in the oven. 4. Take the cake out after an hour. 5. Let the cake cool.

Question	Answer	Common Core Reading Standard
1	D	Determine the meaning of words and phrases as they are used in a text, distinguishing literal from nonliteral language.
2	B	Describe characters in a story (e.g., their traits, motivations, or feelings) and explain how their actions contribute to the sequence of events.
3	C	Ask and answer questions to demonstrate understanding of a text, referring explicitly to the text as the basis for the answers.
4	B	Recount stories; determine the central message, lesson, or moral and explain how it is conveyed through key details in the text.
5	See Below	Refer to parts of stories, dramas, and poems when writing or speaking about a text, using terms such as chapter, scene, and stanza; describe how each successive part builds on earlier sections.

Give a score of 0, 1, 2, 3, or 4 based on how well the answer meets the criteria listed.
- It should describe two things that went wrong and how the narrator will stop it going wrong again.
- It could refer to it being undercooked, not measuring the ingredients, or not letting the cake cool before putting the frosting on.
- It should use relevant details from the passage.
- It should be well-organized, clear, and easy to understand.

Set 10: Literary and Informational Texts

Making Goo

Core Skills Practice
Core skill: Use information gained from illustrations
Answer: The student should explain that the picture helps show what the goo feels like or shows that the goo is slippery or slimy.

Question	Answer	Common Core Reading Standard
1	B	Determine the meaning of general academic and domain-specific words and phrases in a text.
2	B	Describe the logical connection between particular sentences and paragraphs in a text.
3	3, 1, 2, 4	Describe the relationship between a series of historical events, scientific ideas or concepts, or steps in technical procedures in a text, using language that pertains to time, sequence, and cause/effect.
4	C	Ask and answer questions to demonstrate understanding of a text, referring explicitly to the text as the basis for the answers.

Gorillas

Core Skills Practice
Core skill: Determine the meaning of words and phrases in a text
Answer: The student should write a valid definition of each word. Examples are given below.
endangered: An endangered animal is one where there are few of them left.
herbivore: A herbivore is an animal that only eats plants.

Question	Answer	Common Core Reading Standard
1	A	Determine the meaning of general academic and domain-specific words and phrases in a text.
2	C	Use information gained from illustrations and the words in a text to demonstrate understanding of the text.
3	D	Distinguish their own point of view from that of the author of a text.
4	D	Determine the main idea of a text; recount the key details and explain how they support the main idea.

A Happy Day

Core Skills Practice

Core skill: Write an informative text
Answer: The student should write a summary of a book or movie.

Question	Answer	Common Core Reading Standard
1	A	Determine the meaning of words and phrases as they are used in a text, distinguishing literal from nonliteral language.
2	D	Distinguish their own point of view from that of the narrator or those of the characters.
3	C	Ask and answer questions to demonstrate understanding of a text, referring explicitly to the text as the basis for the answers.
4	D	Describe characters in a story (e.g., their traits, motivations, or feelings) and explain how their actions contribute to the sequence of events.

It's Hailing, It's Pouring

Core Skills Practice

Core skill: Use information gained from illustrations
Answer: The student should describe how the photograph shows what size hailstones can be. The student should relate the large size to how much damage a falling hailstone could cause.

Question	Answer	Common Core Reading Standard
1	B	Ask and answer questions to demonstrate understanding of a text, referring explicitly to the text as the basis for the answers.
2	D	Describe the relationship between a series of historical events, scientific ideas or concepts, or steps in technical procedures in a text, using language that pertains to time, sequence, and cause/effect.
3	B	Describe the logical connection between particular sentences and paragraphs in a text.
4	B	Describe the relationship between a series of historical events, scientific ideas or concepts, or steps in technical procedures in a text, using language that pertains to time, sequence, and cause/effect.
5	See Below	Determine the main idea of a text; recount the key details and explain how they support the main idea.

Give a score of 0, 1, 2, 3, or 4 based on how well the answer meets the criteria listed.
- The student should draw a valid conclusion about why hail is dangerous.
- The student may refer to how hail is made of hard ice, how hailstones can be very large, or how they can fall at great speeds.
- The student may describe how people could be hurt if hail hit them. The student may also describe other reasonable dangers such as drivers having accidents because of hail.
- It should use relevant details from the passage.
- It should be well-organized, clear, and easy to understand.

Set 11: Paired Literary Texts

Animals of the Night/Stormy Night

Core Skills Practice
Core skill: Write narratives using descriptive details
Answer: The student should write a narrative describing a scene, and use details to describe the sounds of the scene.

Core Skills Practice
Core skill: Explain how information is conveyed through key details
Answer: The student should complete the table with the details below.
Sight of the sky: dark
Sound of the wind: howling
Sound of the bending trees: creaking
Sound of the windows: rattling

Question	Answer	Common Core Reading Standard
1	B	Determine the meaning of words and phrases as they are used in a text, distinguishing literal from nonliteral language.
2	A	Refer to parts of stories, dramas, and poems when writing or speaking about a text, using terms such as chapter, scene, and stanza; describe how each successive part builds on earlier sections.
3	A	Ask and answer questions to demonstrate understanding of a text, referring explicitly to the text as the basis for the answers.
4	C	Recount stories; determine the central message, lesson, or moral and explain how it is conveyed through key details in the text.
5	C	Recount stories; determine the central message, lesson, or moral and explain how it is conveyed through key details in the text.
6	B	Distinguish their own point of view from that of the narrator or those of the characters.
7	D	Ask and answer questions to demonstrate understanding of a text, referring explicitly to the text as the basis for the answers.
8	C	Determine the meaning of words and phrases as they are used in a text, distinguishing literal from nonliteral language.
9	See Below	Describe characters in a story (e.g., their traits, motivations, or feelings) and explain how their actions contribute to the sequence of events.
10	See Below	Compare and contrast the themes, settings, and plots of stories written by the same author about the same or similar characters.
11	See Below	Compare and contrast the themes, settings, and plots of stories written by the same author about the same or similar characters.
12	See Below	Compare and contrast the themes, settings, and plots of stories written by the same author about the same or similar characters.

Reading Comprehension, Common Core Workbook, Grade 3

Q9.
Give a score of 0, 1, 2, 3, or 4 based on how well the answer meets the criteria listed.
- It should give examples of how Farmer Paul shows kindness.
- It should describe and analyze the actions of Farmer Paul.
- It should use relevant details from the passage.
- It should be well-organized, clear, and easy to understand.

Q10.
Give a score of 0, 1, or 2 based on how well the answer meets the criteria listed.
- It should describe one similarity and one difference between the two settings.
- The similarity could be that they are both set at night or both set in a place where animals are found.
- The difference could be that one is set on a farm and one is set in a city.

Q11.
Give a score of 0, 1, or 2 based on how well the answer meets the criteria listed.
- The student should explain that the animals are given human qualities in "Stormy Night."
- The answer should refer to how the emotions or feelings of the farm animals are described.

Q12.
Give a score of 0, 1, 2, 3, or 4 based on how well the answer meets the criteria listed.
- It should identify that humans are most important to the animals in "Stormy Night."
- The answer should refer to how the farmer has to take care of the animals, while the animals in "Animals of the Night" do not need the humans.
- It should use relevant details from both passages.
- It should be well-organized, clear, and easy to understand.

Set 12: Paired Informational Texts

Recycling is Important/Saving Water

Core Skills Practice
Core skill: Identify supporting details in a text
Answer: The student should complete the chart with the two supporting details below.
- It uses less energy.
- It decreases waste.

Core Skills Practice
Core skill: Form and express an opinion based on a text
Answer: The student should give an opinion on whether or not it is important to save water, and provide reasons to support the opinion.

Question	Answer	Common Core Reading Standard
1	See Below	Ask and answer questions to demonstrate understanding of a text, referring explicitly to the text as the basis for the answers.
2	D	Determine the main idea of a text; recount the key details and explain how they support the main idea.
3	A	Describe the logical connection between particular sentences and paragraphs in a text.
4	B	Use information gained from illustrations and the words in a text to demonstrate understanding of the text.
5	B	Describe the relationship between a series of historical events, scientific ideas or concepts, or steps in technical procedures in a text, using language that pertains to time, sequence, and cause/effect.
6	B	Use text features and search tools (e.g., key words, sidebars, hyperlinks) to locate information relevant to a given topic efficiently.
7	A	Describe the logical connection between particular sentences and paragraphs in a text.
8	A	Determine the main idea of a text; recount the key details and explain how they support the main idea.
9	See Below	Compare and contrast the most important points and key details presented in two texts on the same topic.

Q1.
The student could list any of the following: tin cans, paper, food scraps.

Q9.
Give a score of 0, 1, 2, 3, or 4 based on how well the answer meets the criteria listed.
- It should describe what people can do to help the environment.
- It may refer to reducing trash, recycling items, keeping water clean, or reducing water use.
- It should use relevant details from both passages.
- It should be well-organized, clear, and easy to understand.

Made in the USA
Middletown, DE
09 February 2015